Contents

Introduction

This book is about Database Fundamentals. It will teach you what a database is, what it is used for and why databases are important in the modern day world of Information Technology. More specifically, this book is about Microsoft databases. Microsoft is not the only company that makes database software, and may do things just a bit different from other database software companies (such as Oracle or IBM). However, this is a book for beginners; at this level, the similarities between different database products are much larger than the differences. That means most of what you'll learn will be pretty much the same in the database technology of another vendor.

The intended audience for this book are people who want to learn about databases, for example IT students or IT professionals with a different expertise. At the start of this book, we're going to assume that you know nothing about databases. In fact, you don't need any computer skills at all, except for basic user skills. At the end of this book, you should have a fair working knowledge of databases. This book won't make you an expert, but it will help you on the way. You'll need a lot more studying and years of on-the-job experience to become a database expert, but every expert has to start somewhere, right?

After reading this book and practicing the exercises, you should also be able to pass the Microsoft exam 98-364: Database Fundamentals. This book is not intended as a kind of cram session. Our intention is to teach you the necessary skills and understanding; and as we go along, you'll gain enough knowledge to pass the exam. So if you do not plan on taking this exam, but do want to learn database fundamentals, this is still the right book for you. If you just want to pass the exam and have no interest in actually learning the material, this book is not for you; if we could tell you just the facts you need to know to pass the exams, and nothing more, we wouldn't. We want you to understand the why as well as the how. We will, however, use the objectives of this exam as guideline throughout this book.

This book is divided into six chapters. In chapter 1, we'll begin by installing the database software; in this case, SQL Server 2008 R2. SQL Server is Microsoft's most important database platform. At the moment this book is being written, SQL 2008 R2 is not the latest edition of this software (that is SQL 2014). However, the exam covers SQL 2008, therefore so will we; but the actual version of SQL Server doesn't matter much when it comes to the fundamentals. If you have access to another version (for example, 2005 or 2012), the basics will work pretty much the same as in SQL 2008R2.

After the installation, we'll also create an empty database; without it, we can't do much. Installing SQL Server and creating databases are not exam objectives, so you're not likely to get any questions about this on the exam. However, you need a database to practice on. If you already have an instance of SQL running somewhere, and you can create a database in which you have sufficient permissions (or have one created for you), you can skip this chapter.

Once we have a database to play with, we can start practicing. We'll start with the basic building block of a database: the table. The table is where the actual data gets stored. In chapter 2, we'll show you what a table is, how to put data into it, how to change the data and how to get it out again. This is called manipulating the data.

Going forward, in chapter 3 we'll get to the relational side of things, when we start adding tables. We'll talk about why you'll need multiple tables and how to create relationships between these tables. Also, we'll look at how having multiple tables affects actions like getting data out of these tables.

In chapter 4 we'll talk about other database objects that will help you manipulate the data: views, stored procedures and functions.

Databases have become very important. Most companies nowadays have one or more databases that are called mission critical: without the data, they'd go bankrupt. They need the data, they need it fast and they need to make sure only authorized people have access to the data. This is what the last two chapters are about. In chapter 5, we'll cover what might be the most important thing when it comes to performance: the index. In chapter 6, we'll cover the most important tasks for a database administrator: security (how to give access to the right users, and deny access to everybody else) and backup & restore.

Even though this book starts out easy, SQL Server is a very complex and broad topic. For every general rule, there are a lot of exceptions. So much so, that some people claim that the correct answer to any question about SQL is always: "it depends". But obviously, that answer won't help you. This is especially true in an introductory book like this one. Giving too much details will hinder you, instead of helping you.

So, throughout the book, we'll give you the big picture, and if necessary, come back later with the exceptions. Some exceptions are not important to know at this level, and those exceptions we won't mention at all; this is a study book, not a reference book. For reference, there's Books Online. So we aim for clarity, not for 100% technical correctness. Just to give an example: when talking about backups, we might say that a full backup will allow you to restore the database to the same state as it was at the time you took the backup. This is mostly correct. However, it takes time to perform a backup; for a large database, this might take hours. The contents of the database at the start of the backup may have changed before the end of the backup. So to be 100% correct, instead of mostly correct, we'd have to explain which of those changes are included in the backup, and which changes are not. But to do that, we'd first have to explain a lot of additional concepts (like Log Sequence Numbers, the buffer pool, redo and undo phases). These additional concepts are way out of scope for this book. So we'll skip those concept, ignore the changes that may occur during the backup, and in general, just give you the big picture. If you understand the big picture, you can look up the details and exceptions in Books Online.

About the exam

The Microsoft exam 98-364: Database Fundamentals is one of a series of entry level exams on Microsoft technologies. The exam consists of several multiple choice questions. If you pass the exam, you can call yourself Microsoft Technology Associate (MTA). For more details on the exam, and how to schedule the exam, go to the Microsoft web site. At the time of writing this book, this was the direct link to the web page:

http://www.microsoft.com/learning/en/us/exam.aspx?ID=98-364

Here, Microsoft makes two important statements we want to bring to your attention. The first is: "This objective may include but is not limited to...". This phrase is used for most objectives. The second is: "This preparation guide is subject to change at any time without prior notice and at the sole discretion of Microsoft". So you won't know up front what might be asked on the exam. For you as a student, this means that you must practice, not just the questions and exercises in this book. And review the list of exam objectives on this web site, as it may have changed since the writing of this book.

This exam is the first of several Microsoft exams on SQL Server. So if you find you enjoy working with databases, you can go on to become MCSA (Microsoft Certified Solutions Associate) or MCSE (Microsoft Certified Solutions Expert). Next in line, however, would be exams 70-461 for SQL 2012 database development, or 70-462 for SQL 2012 database administration (at this level, the SQL version does become important).

About the author

Robert is an independent IT consultant, with over 15 years of IT experience. Starting as system engineer, he was introduced to a wide variety of hardware and software, among which SQL Server (at that time: version 7.0). He found that he liked working with databases; both the complexity of the technology and the importance of data to the business processes appealed to him, and still does. That's why he decided to specialize in SQL Server. Since then, he has held a number of database related roles: consultant, engineer, architect and database administrator.

About the method: PQRST

When studying this book, we recommend using the PQRST learning method: Preview, Question, Read, Summarize, Test. This method consists of the following steps:
* Preview. At the start of each chapter, flip through the pages to get an idea of the topics that will be covered. To support this, we'll give a chapter overview and mention some key concepts that will be covered.
* Question. At the beginning of each chapter, we'll post some questions you should be able to answer after reading the chapter. Think of additional questions you might have about these topics: "why does it work this way? Why not do it like that?". Maybe you have encountered relevant situations in your past. We advise you to actually write these questions down.
* Read. This should be obvious.
* Summarize. After reading each chapter, we'll give a summary. It is a good idea to make your own summary before reading ours, and then compare notes.
* Test. See if you can answer the questions provided, especially your own. That's why we recommend writing them down before you start reading.

Just reading is not the best way to memorize material. Actually formulating your own questions about the material beforehand, and seeing if you can answer your own questions afterwards, will make you a much more active participant. This will help you remember the material. If you're unable to answer your questions, or if you have additional questions, look them up online. Or post the questions on a SQL server related web site.
Of course, you'll also have to practice writing SQL code. A lot. So let's get started.

Chapter 1: Installing SQL Server

Chapter overview

In this chapter, we'll perform a very basic installation of SQL Server 2008 R2. Then, we'll take a short tour of the most important tool used to manage SQL Server: SQL Server Management Studio (SSMS). The last thing we'll do in this chapter is create a database. You won't need to know any of this for the exam, but you do need to have an actual database to be able to perform the exercises in the rest of this book.

These three subjects (installation, SQL Management Studio & creating a database) are very broad subjects. There will be a lot of options we won't discuss, or only glance over. Explaining all of these options takes several extra books. Just don't get intimidated when you see the number of options in the SQL installation process.

Key concepts
SSMS, GUI, instance, query window, Object Explorer

Requirements
* SQL Server trial software (available for download on http://www.microsoft.com/en-us/download/default.aspx);
* a pc or a server that is powerful enough to install SQL Server on. Microsoft states the minimum requirements as:
>   * Supported operating systems: Windows Server 2003 Service Pack 2, Windows Server 2008, Windows Vista, Windows Vista Service Pack 1, Windows XP Service Pack 2, Windows XP Service Pack 3
>   * 32-bit systems: Computer with Intel or compatible 1GHz or faster processor (2 GHz or faster is recommended.)
>   * 64-bit systems: 1.4 GHz or higher processor
>   * Minimum of 512 MB of RAM (2 GB or more is recommended.)
>   * 2.2 GB of available hard disk space
* Adventureworks sample database (available for download on http://msftdbprodsamples.codeplex.com/)

Exam objectives
For the exam, the relevant objectives are: none. Therefore, no questions.

Installation

Preparing the installation
Before installing SQL Server, you have to prepare the installation. In our case, this means the following:
* Making sure the pc you're installing on meets the minimum requirements, as stated above;
* Download the SQL Server trial software from the Microsoft site. This is a fully functional version that you can use free-of-charge for 180 days, as long as you only use it for testing purposes. Here, we've used SQL 2008R2 (R2 means Release 2; this might be a bit confusing, as release 1 is just called 2008, not 2008 R1).

If you have a pc that is powerful enough, we recommend installing SQL Server on a virtual machine. This is a very good way of testing installations, because after you're done, you can discard the virtual machine. This is a far more effective way of removing SQL Server than uninstall, because despite its name, an uninstall will not completely uninstall everything. In the process of writing this book, we've used Oracle VirtualBox to create a virtual machine with Windows Server 2008. VirtualBox is a free tool, available from Oracle. For more information on using VirtualBox, look up Oracle VirtualBox in your favorite search engine. Just like SQL Server, Windows Server is available as free trial software from Microsoft.

Another benefit of using a virtual machine is that you can install a clean version of Windows on this virtual machine, before installing SQL. Performing a basic installation of SQL is pretty easy on a clean Windows environment, but unexpected errors can occur if some Windows components have been removed or are being blocked by security software; also, other applications may get in the way of installing SQL Server. Using a virtual machine may sound complicated if you've never done this, but it's actually pretty straightforward. If you don't feel up to this task at the moment, just install SQL directly on your local computer.

In performing this test installation, we'll make some choices you wouldn't make for an installation that would actually be used in production; such an installation would require more preparation. We'll mention some of those preparations, just to give you an idea of the tasks a database administrator faces:

* Estimating the actual requirements your database(s) are going to need, as these are probably way more than the minimum requirements (whereas the minimum requirements are a 1 GHz processor, 2.2 GB of free space and 512 MB of RAM, a database for 20 thousand users might need 4 quad core CPU's, 128 GB of RAM, and a terabyte of disk space on lots of blazingly fast disks);
* Choosing which SQL components are needed (from the long list of available components);
* Reviewing each possible setting for each component and choosing the right one;
* Designing and testing a high availability & disaster recovery strategy that meets the Service Level Agreement for the application;
* Documenting the entire installation process. It might seem odd to list this under "Preparing the installation". However, unless you only install SQL once in an environment, we believe it is best to create a document describing the company standard for a SQL Server installation. Then, for an actual installation, you only have to document the steps where you purposely deviate from this company standard. Creating this company standard is preparation.
* Choosing the right version (i.e. 2008, 2008R2, 2012, 2014) and edition (e.g. Standard, Enterprise, Express or Developer), and purchasing the licenses;
* Choosing the right service pack and patch level, based on your company policy and the applications compatibility;
* Creating separate service accounts for each service that is going to be installed.

Don't worry if not everything on this list makes sense. Just know that, based on the business requirements, this list can be a lot longer. Preparing for the installation should take a lot longer than the actual installation. Remember the old adage: an ounce of prevention is worth a pound of cure. If you find out your server isn't fit for purpose when the application is already "live" and being used by thousands of users, these users will not be happy if you have to take the database offline to correct mistakes. However, it is quite easy to install SQL in a way that is fit for the purpose of this book, so let's get busy.

Installing SQL Server

To most readers, looking at screenshots of an installation is as boring as watching paint dry, so we've posted a video of the installation online. This video can be found on the authors blog: http://www.rbvandenberg.com/mta-98-364/installing-sql-server-2008-r2/

A few notes on the installation that should have made the video, but didn't:
* *Collation* determines the sort order and comparison of characters. For example, one difference between collations is whether it is case sensitive or case insensitive. In a *case insensitive* collation, "e" equals "E", but in a *case sensitive* database, "e" does not equal "E"; in an *accent insensitive* database, "e" equals "é", but in an *accent sensitive* database, it does not.
* The general recommendation for service accounts is to create a different domain account for each service.

After watching the video, you can jump to the next section, **Troubleshooting the installation**. The remainder of this section is intended for those of you who can't watch the video online, or prefer to look at screenshots.

A note up front: at certain times during the setup procedure, there will be no visible sign of progress, sometimes even for minutes if your pc is a bit slow. This is normal.

Now, let's get started:
* Download the evaluation edition of SQL Server 2008 R2 from the Microsoft web site to a folder on your local hard drive;
* Double click the executable;

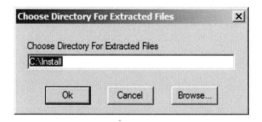

* Choose a directory to extract all files to (this may take a minute or so, depending on the speed of your hard drive);
* After you see the "extraction complete" message, browse to the directory and double click setup.exe;

* Depending on the configuration of you pc, you may or may not get the message that the .Net framework has to be installed. If you receive this message, click OK. This is one of those actions that may take some time, without any visible progress.
* After a while, the *SQL Server Installation Center* screen will appear.

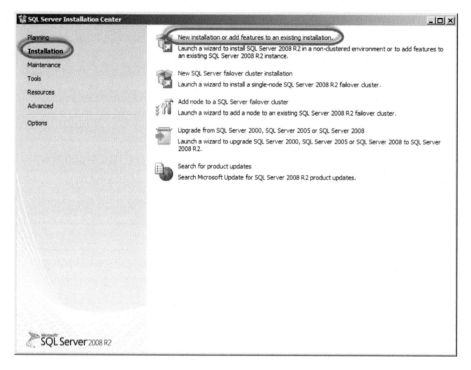

* Click **Installation** , followed by **New installation or add features to an existing installation**.
* The *SQL Server 2008 R2 Setup* screen will appear.

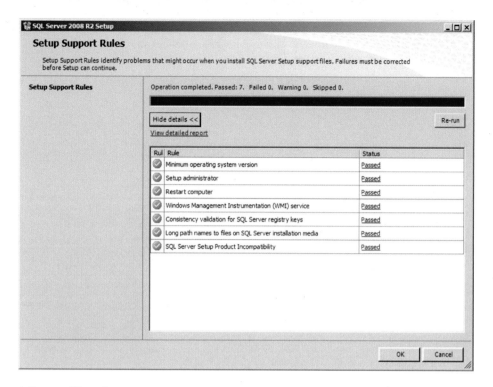

* Setup will perform some checks. Click **Show details** to see what checks are performed, and the result. If all checks have passed, click **OK** to proceed (again, with a delay that may take a minute).

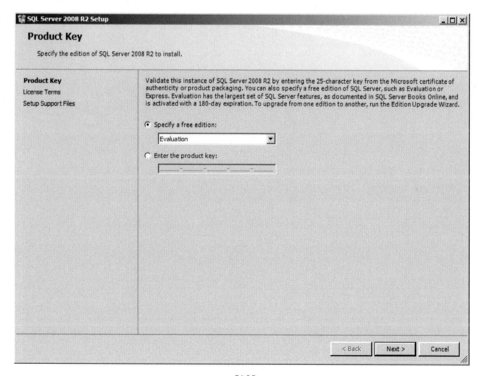

* In the *Product Key* screen, enter a valid product key, or choose to install an evaluation edition. An evaluation edition will provide the same features as an Enterprise edition. Click **Next**.

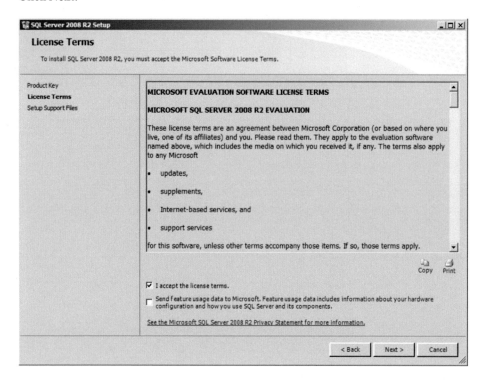

* On the *License Terms* screen, check the box next to "I accept the license terms.". Click **Next**.

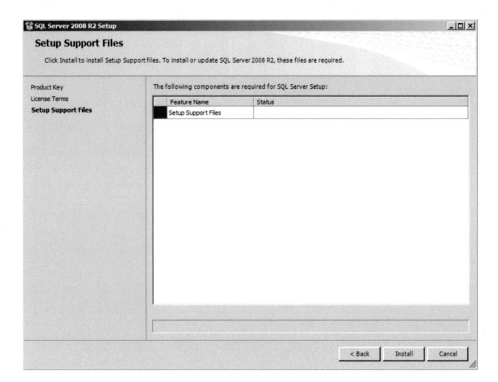

* The next screen is the *Setup Support Rules* screen. This will show the result of some additional checks, based on the edition you've chosen. If you receive any warnings, please make sure that you understand the impact of the warning before you proceed. Otherwise, you may run into trouble later on. In this case, we got two warnings: Windows firewall is on, which may prevent other computers from reaching this SQL Server, and a .Net application warning, caused by the fact that this server isn't connected to the internet. Neither will cause problems later on, so we can proceed. Click **Next**.

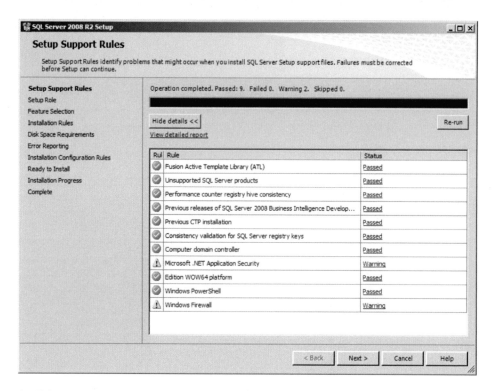

* Click **Install** on the *Setup support files* screen. Click **Next**.

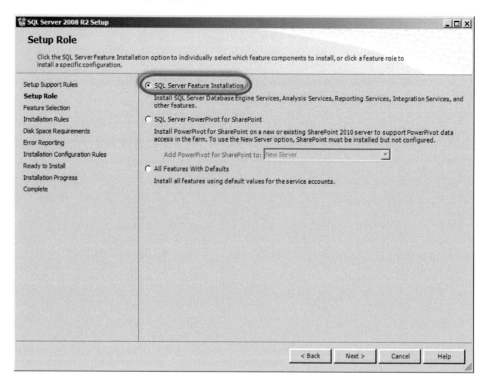

* Choose the default, "SQL Server Feature Installation". Option number two is intended for SharePoint, and we're not using SharePoint. Option number three would install all features with their defaults, which includes a lot of features we don't need, and that is never a good idea. Click **Next**.

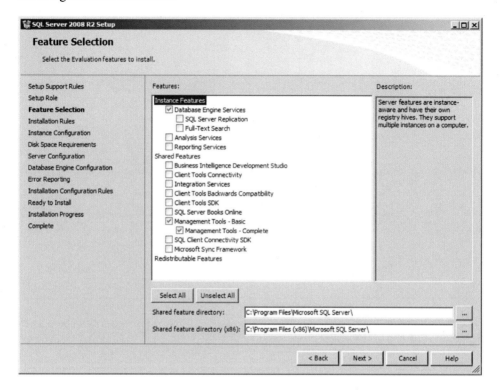

* In the *Feature selection* screen, choose only the features you need: *Database engine services* and *Management tools – complete*. If you want, you can also install the SQL Server help files, called Books Online. There is a good reason not to install every single feature: features that aren't installed do not use any resources, do not need to be patched and cannot be hacked. On a production server, you might choose to install only *Database engine services,* and choose to install Management Studio on a separate workstation. Click **Next**.

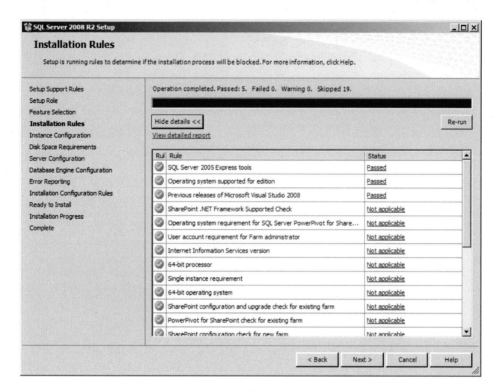

* An additional set of rules, relevant to your choices in the *Feature selection* screen, will be checked. If every check is passed: click **Next**.

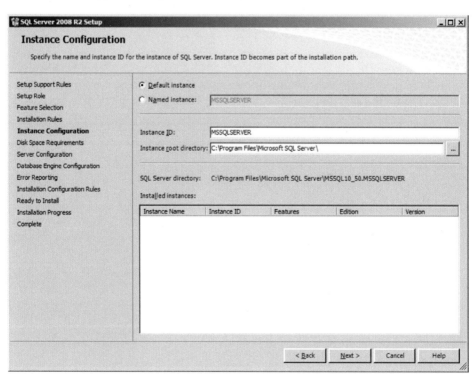

* We will only be installing a single instance, and this will be a default instance. On a single server, you can install one default instance, and several named instances, for a total of up to 50 instances. An instance is a completely isolated installation of SQL Server, with its own files, processes and TCP/IP port number. The difference between a named instance and a default instance is that, in order to connect to a default instance, you only have to provide the server name, and in order to connect to a named instance, you have to provide both the server and instance name. So here, we'll leave the defaults, and click **Next**.

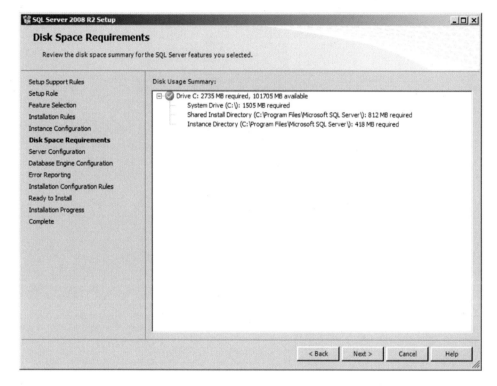

* On the *Disk space requirements* screen, you can see how much disk space your selection of features requires. Click **Next**.

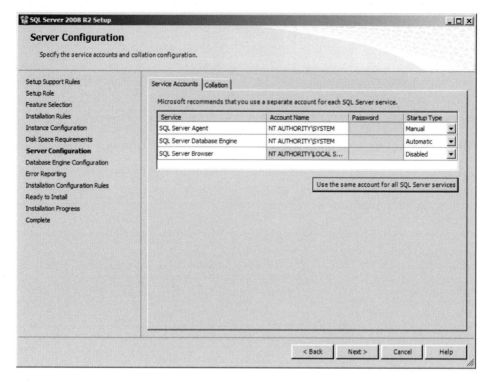

* The *Server configuration* screen has two tabs: *service accounts* and *collation*.
Collation determines the sort order and comparison of characters. For example, one
difference between collations is whether it is case sensitive or case insensitive. In a *case
insensitive* collation, "e" equals "E", but in a *case sensitive* database, "e" does not equal
"E"; in an *accent insensitive* database, "e" equals "é", but in an *accent sensitive*
database, it does not. Here, we've chosen the default:
SQL_Latin1_General_CP1_CI_AS.
On the *Service* accounts tab, you have to choose a service account for each of the three
services: the database engine, the SQL agent and the browser. If you've selected more
features to install, you may see more services in this list.
A service is a program that runs in the background. The database engine service is the
main SQL program, that controls all access to the database files. This service needs to
run at all times; therefore, the startup type is automatic, meaning that this service will
start up when the server starts up. The SQL Agent is a task scheduler that performs tasks
at certain times, for example to perform maintenance jobs such as backups. Since our
test server doesn't need to perform scheduled backups, the startup type for this service
can be left at the default: manual (meaning it won't start until someone manually starts
the service). The third service is needed for named instances. As mentioned before, each
instance runs on its own TCP/IP port. The default instance will run on port 1433; a
named instance will run, by default, on a random port, in which case the browser service
is needed to inform a client computer on which port this named instance is running.
Since we won't use a named instance, we do not need the browser service, and can
therefore leave the startup type at its default: disabled.
The general recommendation for service accounts is to create a different domain account
for each service. Here, we choose the local system account, as this SQL Server will not
be initiating actions to other servers. This service account can be changed later on, after
the installation; collation cannot be changed without reinstalling the SQL instance.

[20]

After configuring all the required settings, click **Next**.

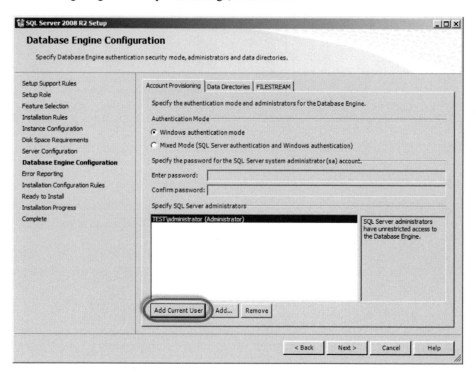

The *Database engine configuration* screen has three tabs: *Account provisioning*, *Data directories* and *filestream*.

On the *Account provisioning* tab, you specify which accounts will be granted initial access to SQL Server. You can provide additional accounts once SQL is installed. There are two types of accounts: SQL accounts and Windows accounts. If you choose Windows authentication mode, which is the default, you can only grant Windows accounts access to SQL Server; the alternative, mixed mode, allows for both Windows and SQL accounts. This does not yet grant anybody access; it just allows for either one or both types to be granted access later on. SQL is secure by default, meaning that no one has access until their account has been explicitly granted access by a SQL administrator.

The reason that Windows authentication is the default, is that it is more secure and easier to maintain. However, many applications require a SQL account, so most SQL instances in the real world are configured as mixed mode. In the case of mixed mode, we need to provide a password for the sa account, which is the SQL administrator (also called sysadmin). If you choose Windows authentication, it is necessary to add the current user as a SQL administrator, otherwise you won't be able to logon after installation. We'll cover security in greater detail in the final chapters of this book.

On the *Data directories* tab, you provide the path for different types of files: system files, database files, log files and backup files. Depending on your hardware, you can get significant performance gains by separating different files on different hard drives. In a production environment, you may spend a lot of time testing and analyzing the optimal configuration for your server; on this test server, we only have a C drive, so all files will be placed there. Besides performance, there is another reason why it is absolutely not

done to put your database files on your C drive in a production environment: your database files can fill up your entire C drive, crashing your server.
The final tab is for filestream, but we won't be using that.

* On the *Error reporting* screen (not shown), you can choose to send error report to Microsoft. Click **Next**.

* On the *Installation configuration rules* screen, a final set of checks are performed. Click **Next**.

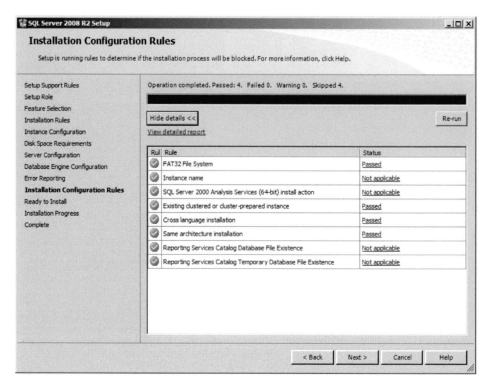

* On the *Ready to install* screen, you get a final chance to review all the choices you have made. Review the list, then click **Install**.

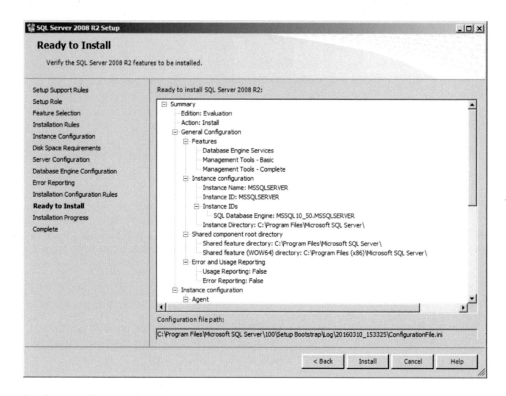

* After a while, you should get a message informing you that SQL has been installed successfully.

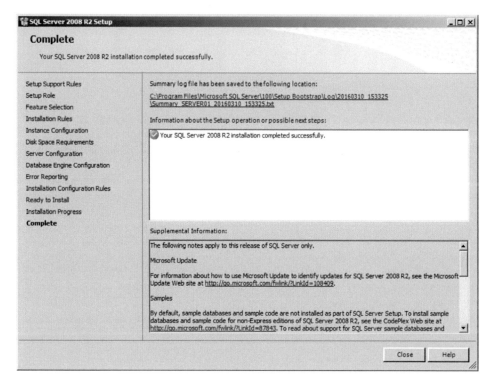

Troubleshooting the installation

Hopefully, you've encountered no difficulties during the installation. If so, you can skip this part. If not, you'll have to fix the installation. The first place to start is the error message you get. If this error message doesn't give you an idea how to fix the problem, paste the error message in your favorite search engine. There are a lot of excellent SQL Server support sites out there.

The next resource to find out what went wrong is the Event Viewer. You can find this at the following location: *Start > Administrative Tools > Event Viewer*. Check the *Application Log* for errors.

The final place to look is the SQL Server setup log. This is located in *C:\program files\Microsoft SQL Server\100\Setup Bootstrap\Log*. There will be a *Summary.txt* file, and at least two directories: one for the setup support files and one for SQL Server, each with a timestamp as their name. The summary file should point you to the log file of the part of the installation that went wrong. The bad news is that these files are very detailed, and therefore not easy to read; the good news is that, because these files are very detailed, the error is probably in there.

After the installation

For the purpose of this book, we're finished with the installation. In the real world, there are several more things that have to be done. Just as with the preparation, we'll mention some of these actions to give you an idea of the activities of a DBA:
* Install the latest service pack and patches;
* Read through the error logs, to see if there have been issues that may not have been severe enough to hinder the installation, but have to be resolved anyway;
* Configure SQL Server settings and services;
* Configure backups and other maintenance jobs;
* Run performance tests to see if the disks are fast enough for the workload you intend to run;
* Install and configure a monitoring tool.

We'll skip those activities, and move on to the next part.

A short tour of SSMS

SQL Server Management Studio (SSMS) is the tool most often used to manage SQL Server. There are other tools to manage SQL Server, but SSMS is provided for free by Microsoft, and powerful enough for most purposes.

Before we go on, it might be useful to point out that SSMS is a completely separate program from the SQL Server database engine. SSMS is just one program that can connect to the database engine and perform database requests, just as any other program can. The actual database engine is sqlserver.exe. This is the program that controls & locks the database files, ensuring that every access to the databases has to be performed through the database engine.

To start up SSMS, go to *Start > Programs > Microsoft SQL Server 2008 R2 > SQL Server Management Studio*. Obviously, if you've installed SQL 2008 instead of 2008 R2, this path is slightly different.

The next screen you'll see should be the "Connect to server" screen, and it should look something like this:

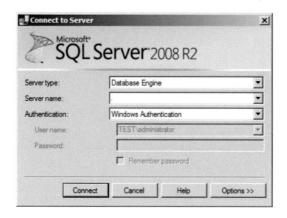

Here, specify the following information:
* Server type: Database Engine.
* Server name: the name of your SQL Server instance. This takes the form of "server name\instance name", or, in the case of a default instance, of "server name". We've installed a default instance, so enter the name of your computer, or just a single period (".").
* Authentication: either "SQL Server Authentication" or "Windows Authentication". During the installation, in the "Database Engine Configuration" screen, we chose "Windows authentication mode", so we can't connect using "SQL Server Authentication". In the same setup screen, we clicked the button "Add current user", so if you did the same, your Windows account has been granted access. Each SQL Server instance is configured, during installation, with either "mixed mode" or "Windows authentication mode". "Mixed mode" means SQL allows both "SQL Server Authentication" and "Windows authentication". More on this in chapter 6.

Click Connect. SSMS should now open with, on the left, the Object explorer. Notice the drop down arrow, the pin and the cross to the right of the words Object Explorer. With this, you can close or move the Object Explorer.

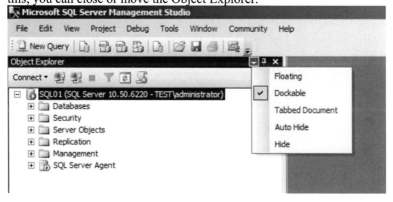

If you press the pin, the Object Explorer will "auto hide", and collapse to the side (leaving only a small label).

You can make the Object Explorer reappear by either clicking on the label, by using keyboard shortcut F8 or from the View menu. Pressing the pin again disables this "auto hide" behavior. For example, you can choose "Floating" for the object explorer and move it outside of the main SSMS screen; this works especially well if you want to use multiple monitors.

In the Object Explorer, you can browse some aspects of your SQL Server instance:
* Databases, divided into system databases and user databases;
* Security, where you can find (among other things) what logins have been granted permission;
* Server objects, Replication and Management;
* SQL Server Agent, where you can find scheduled jobs and set up alerts.

For this book you'll only need to browse Databases and Security.

Please play around with the docking, floating and hiding of the Object Explorer and the other tabs, such as Registered Servers, Template Explorer and Object Explorer Details; it is far easier to understand the behavior of the various options by experimenting with them, than by reading about them. As you move through the chapters of this book, play with these windows and find a setup that works for you.

The amount of available tools and windows is overwhelming at first, and if you display them all, this will clutter even the largest monitor. Therefore, it is important to find a setup that works for you. For now, let's move on to the most important window: the Query window.

You can open a new query window in a number of different ways:
* From the File menu, using "Query with Current Connection". The keyboard shortcut for this is CTRL + N (see screenshot below).
* From the File menu, using "Database Engine Query". You'll be asked to make a new connection.
* By opening a saved SQL file. This will open a query window with the current database connection (i.e. the same SQL instance, the same database and the same Windows or SQL user credentials).

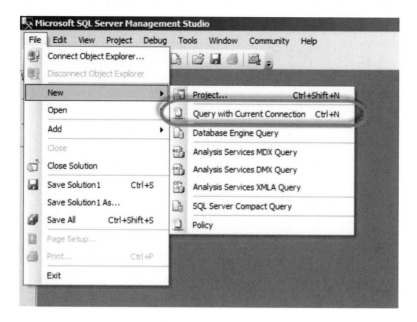

These connection details can be seen at the bottom of each query window:
* The connection status, either connected or disconnected;
* The name of the SQL Server instance, and its version (including service pack level);
* The account you're connected with (either SQL or Windows), and the id of your session;
* The database you're connected to;
* The number of records affected by the last query, and its duration.

By the way: you can set the color of the status bar in the "Connection Properties" tab of the "Connect to database Engine" screen. This can be quite convenient when you have lots of SQL instances; you can use a different color for different instances, or a different color for production and test instances. This decreases the change that you perform a query on the wrong server (you wouldn't be the first to accidentally run a test script on a production server).

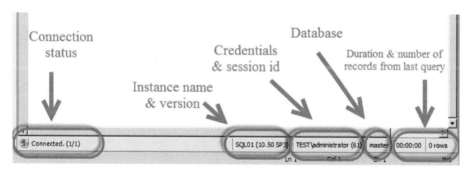

You can also see the database connection in the upper left corner. Using the arrow next to the database name, you can select which database you're connected to. The keyboard shortcut for this is ALT + D.

These connection details, and more, can be seen in the Properties Window as well:

Please note that some screenshots have been made using different SQL instances, so things like build number might change from one screenshot to the next.

The keyboard shortcut for the Properties window is F4. You can have many query windows open at the same time, each with its own connection. By dragging the tab labels, you can drag them around to meet your needs.

Right click on the label and click "New Vertical Tab Group" to get two query windows side-by-side:

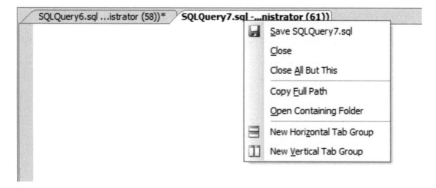

For this book, we've put a number before query lines for easy reference. You can enable line numbers by going to *Tools > Options*, and selecting the appropriate check box (under *Text Editor > Transact-SQL > General*).

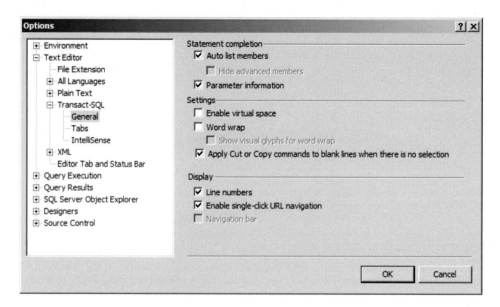

Now let's start typing our first query. We haven't created a database yet, so connect to system database "master". Type the following query "SELEKT GETDATE()". This should tell us the current date and time. However, this doesn't work:

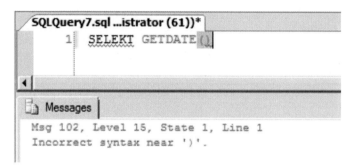

This query contains a typo; SELEKT should be spelled as SELECT. See the red line underneath the text? Management Studio does spell checking while you type; this is called Intellisense. Move your cursor over the red line, and SQL will tell you what it thinks is wrong with the code. In this case, it will tell you: "couldn't find stored procedure 'selekt'"; Intellisense wrongly assumes you're referring to a stored procedure. More on stored procedures in chapter 4.

Intellisense checks the correct spelling of SQL keywords and user objects, as well as the correct syntax of entire SQL statements. It also makes suggestions while you type:

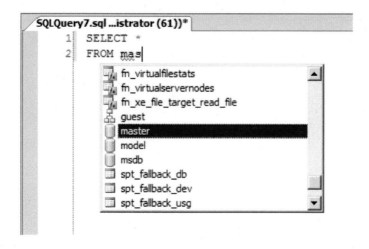

By pressing TAB you can confirm the suggestion, and Intellisense will complete the word for you. Auto completion and syntax checking can save you a lot of time while programming. At times, you may find that you've just created an object, but Intellisense insists that the object doesn't exist. That is because Intellisense doesn't automatically "know" what objects are available in real time; it has to query the database and ask what objects are available. By pressing CTRL+SHIFT+R you can instruct Intellisense to perform this query again, thereby refreshing the Intellisense cache. At the start of this short tour we said that SSMS is not the database engine itself, but just a program connecting to the database engine; this is one example that demonstrates this difference. The last SSMS trick we want to tell you about is Books Online, or BOL as it is often called. This is local help. Press F1 to open Books Online. The first time you use Books Online, you have to choose whether to use Books Online on the internet, or on your local computer; the latter option is probably faster. Not every application has a help file that is actually very helpful, but Books Online is definitely helpful. It is both very complete and very accurate.

One particularly useful feature is context sensitive help. Highlight any keyword in a query window and press F1; Books Online will open the page relevant to that keyword, complete with all options and code samples.

One more thing before we'll move on to creating a database: keyboard shortcuts. Learning to use keyboard shortcuts (instead of using your mouse) is time well spent. You do not *need* to know these keyboard shortcuts, but if you do learn to use them, you'll be able to work a lot faster.

Shortcut	Context	Action
ALT + D	Query Window	Change database
CTRL + N	Object Explorer/Query window	Opens new query window
F5	Object Explorer	Refresh
F5	Query Window	Execute selected code
CTRL + F5	Query Window	Perform syntax check on selected code
F8	Object Explorer	Jump to Object Explorer
CTRL + F4	Query Window	Close query window
CTRL + R	Query Window	Show/hide result pane

Two notes about these shortcuts. Pressing F5 in the query window will execute the selected code; if no code is selected, all code in the window will be executed. Refreshing, by pressing F5 in the object explorer, will not refresh the list of all types of objects. For example, if you press F5 when "Tables" is selected, SSMS will refresh the list of tables in this database, but not the list of databases on this particular SQL instance.

This is a list of some of the keyboard shortcuts that are available in SQL Server Management Studio. For an exhaustive list, see the Microsoft web site: http://msdn.microsoft.com/en-us/library/ms174205.aspx

Creating a database

For the rest of this book, we'll be needing two databases: an empty database and a database with sample data. The sample database will be used throughout the remainder of the book for the exercises; the empty database will be used to create our own samples. We'll create the empty database from SSMS, and the sample database from backup. To create an empty database, go to the Object Explorer in SSMS and right click Databases.

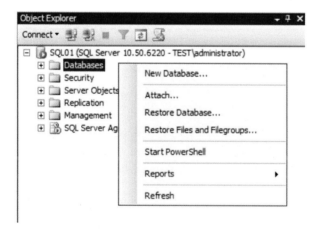

Click "New Database". In the "New Database" screen, enter the name "testdatabase", and click "OK".

That's it. In real life, there are a lot of concerns we have to think about when creating databases, such as file placement, sizing and maintenance; all of that is not relevant here. Now let's move on to the next database. Microsoft provides a sample database but for SQL 2008, unlike older SQL versions, this sample database is not installed by default. To do this, we need to download this sample database from the Codeplex web site, on: http://msftdbprodsamples.codeplex.com/ . Unfortunately, this database (called AdventureWorks) is available in many different versions at the time of writing:
* SQL version: 2008, 2008R2, 2012, 2014 or SQL Azure;
* OLTP or DW version;
* Full or lite version;
* Script, file or backup.

You'll need the backup of the full OLTP version for the SQL version you have installed. If this file has been moved to a different location on the Codeplex web site, you can search for "AdventureWorks2008R2-Full Database Backup.zip" in your favorite search engine.

To load up this database, perform the following actions:
* Download this zip file. The zip file contains a backup file (with an extension of BAK),
named "AdventureWorks2008R2-Full Database Backup.bak".
* Extract/unzip this file to your local computer.
* Open SSMS.
* In Object Explorer, right click "Databases".
* Choose "Restore Database".
* Click "From device".
* Click the ellipsis button (…). This opens the "Specify backup" screen.
* Click "Add". Browse to the file you've just extracted.

Check the box. A single backup file can contain multiple backups, but this backup file
contains only one.
For "To database:", enter the database name. Or, select it from the drop down box. The
screen should now look like this:

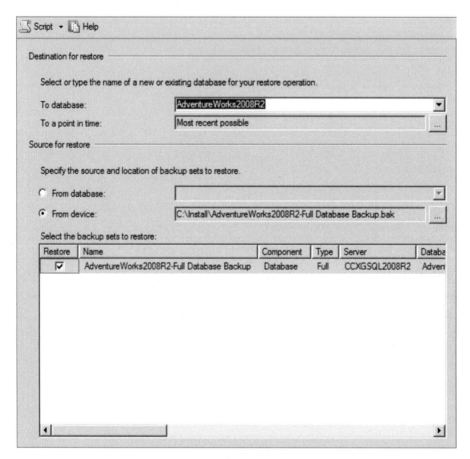

Click "OK".
SQL will now create a new database called AdventureWorks2008R2 from the backup
file. This may take a minute or so. After this, we've got a working database to play with,
and we're ready to learn some database fundamentals.

Summary

In this chapter, we've done some preliminary work for the rest of this book. We've performed an installation of SQL Server 2008. We've installed only the necessary features, and made some choices that are probably not secure enough for a production environment. Having installed SQL Server, we've done a short tour of the program you'll have the most interaction with: SQL Server Management Studio, or SSMS. You've seen how to connect to SQL Server, how to browse the databases and objects, and how to customize the various windows. Finally, we've created two databases: an empty databases for the code samples we're going to use in the text of the next chapters, and the AdventureWorks database with sample data for the exercises.

This is not material you'll need for the exam, so we've covered these subjects in just enough detail to help you through the rest of this book.

Further reading
None

Test
There are no exam objectives for the installation of SQL Server, therefore there were no questions at the beginning of this chapter.

Chapter 2: Using a single table

Chapter overview

Preview
In this chapter, we'll talk about what a database is, and about the most important part of the database: the table. Before we can actually create a table in SQL, you need to know some terms and aspects, so we'll cover those. Then we'll show you two ways of creating a table: using the graphical interface and using a script. Once we have a table, we'll cover how to put data into that table, read data from the table, change the data & delete it from the table.

Key concepts
table, row, column, data type, null, Transact-SQL, DDL, DML, CREATE, DROP, SELECT, INSERT, UPDATE, DELETE

Requirements
You need access to a test database with database owner (dbo) privileges, like the one we created in chapter 1.

Exam objectives
For the exam, the relevant objectives are:
* Understanding what a table is and how it relates to the data that will be stored in the database; columns/fields, rows/records
* Understand data manipulation language (DML) and its role in databases
* Understand data definition language (DDL). understanding how T-SQL can be used to create database objects such as tables and views
* Choose data types. understanding what data types are, why they are important, and how they affect storage requirements
* Understand tables and how to create them.
* Purpose of tables; creating tables in a database by using proper ANSI SQL syntax
* Selecting, inserting, updating, or deleting data

What is a database?

As the name suggests, a database is a piece of software to store data. A database is not intended to store files (for example: Word documents or MP3 files). You can, but that is not what it is designed for. It is designed to store information like sales records or customer information. A PDF document for a sales order has a layout, and would probably include a company logo (in addition to the information about the sales); inside a sales database, you'd only store the data that customer A bought product B (on a certain date for a certain price etc.), but no layout.

So a database stores data, or more specifically: structured data. Before you can store data, you have to define what information you can store there. For example: in an electronic address book, you can probably store "name" and "address", but probably not "hair color". If you want to store "hair color", you have to change the design of the database.

What are the advantages of storing data in a database, as opposed to (for example) a Word file? Database systems are optimized for storing and retrieving data both very fast and very securely, for many users at the same time. Just to clarify: SQL Server is not a database; it is a Relational Database Management System (RDBMS). That means that it is a complete system for databases, and everything surrounding it. SQL Server controls access to the database, backups, file management tasks and other management tasks. So, SQL Server is not a database; it contains databases. We'll go deeper into database systems in chapter 3.

Table

The most important object in a database is the table. A table contains the data, in rows and columns. It looks just like a spreadsheet. This is a very simple example of a table:

First name	Last name	Address
John	Smith	First Street 1, Washington
Peter	Jones	Second Street 2, London
Frank	James	Champs-Elysees, Paris
Jim	Gray	Main Street 7, New York

This is the table we'll create later on in this chapter. It has data about four people. Information about each person is stored in its own row, so there are four rows, called records. There are three columns: First name, Last name and Address. These are also called fields or attributes.

A single table contains information about a single entity. The table in the example contains information about the entity "Person". In chapter 3, we'll go into more detail about how and when to create additional tables, what information to put in the same table and what data to put in different tables; for now, it is enough to know that we'd not put product and sales information in this "Person" table; a sale is a different entity, and so is a product.

In the real world, "Address" would not be a single field; it would be split into several fields: street, house number, house number addition, city, zip code, country and maybe something like district, province or region. Selecting all people living in New York is a lot more difficult (both for the programmer and SQL Server) when the address is stored in a single field, compared to when city is stored as a separate field. But in this example, splitting up address into multiple fields doesn't add any value, so we'll put address into a single field.

Before we can create this table, there are two more things you need to know about attributes: data types and nullability. These are things you need to tell SQL when creating the table, so you need to know what they mean. There are a lot of other settings that can be defined on a table or on an attribute when you create a table, but data type and nullability are required, so we'll cover them first; we'll cover some of the other options later.

Data types

For every attribute, you have to tell SQL what type of data it is: for example, some sort of number, a text string, or a date. Making SQL aware of the data type has several advantages. By defining the data type, you have some defense against users putting data in the wrong field, because you can't put a name in a field that has been defined as a date field. You also can't insert a non-existing date like "February 31, 2000"; SQL would prevent this, and raise an error:

The conversion of a varchar data type to a datetime data type resulted in an out-of-range value.

In addition: SQL handles different data types differently. For example, SQL allows you to easily add one month to "January 31, 2000" if you store this as a date, but if you store it as text, you have to write your own logic to achieve this; it that case, you'd have to make sure that you don't end up with "February 31, 2000". More on this in chapter 4 when we talk about functions.

Another example of how SQL handles different data types differently, is the Boolean. This is basically a field that is either true or false; think of it as a checkbox. An example in an employee database would be an attribute on an employee to indicate whether an employee is a current or a past employee. You could define a text field for this, call it "IsCurrentEmployee", and store either the text string "true" or the text string "false". The better alternative is storing it as a Boolean. As with the date example above, choosing the Boolean as data type limits the possible values to true and false; if you choose a text data type, any value could be entered, including values that don't make sense for that particular attribute.

Also: storing the text string "false" takes at least 5 bytes; storing a Boolean takes only one bit. One byte is 8 bits, so storing "false" as a text string takes up 40 times as much space as storing it as a Boolean.

Five bytes might not seem important, in a time when hard drives are measured in terabytes, but trust me: it is important in database design. These 5 bytes are not just stored on disk, but also in every backup of the database and in the internal memory (RAM) of the server. Nowadays, even server memory is not that expensive anymore, but most database servers don't have enough of it, and memory is often a critical aspect of performance. And those 5 bytes have to be stored for every record; so in a table with a million rows, it wastes 5 MB. And a million rows in a table is not at all uncommon. On a higher level: it is really important to pay attention to details when designing a database. Choosing the smallest data type possible is just one of these details.

But which data type do you have to choose? SQL has a long list of them. You can find a complete list of data types in Books Online; just search for "Data Types (Transact-SQL)". If there is no data type that meets your needs, you can even create your own data type; this is often done for attributes like telephone number or zip code. These are some of the more common data types that are available out-of-the-box:

Category	Data type	Description
Exact numerics	int	Integer: a whole number between
		-2,147,483,648 and 2,147,483,647
	tinyint	Integer: a whole number between 0 and 255
	smallint	Integer: a whole number between -32,768 and 32767
	bigint	Integer: a whole number between
		(-9,223,372,036,854,775,808 and 9223372036854770000
Approximate numeric	Decimal	A number with decimals. Can store aA number with decimals. Can store a maximum of 38 digits. Declared as decimal(p,s), with p as the total number of digits stored and s as the maximum number of digits stored to the right of the decimal point. E.g. dec(5,2) can store the number "123.45"
Date and time	datetime	This data type combines the date and the time
	date	Date
	time	Time
Character strings	char	A fixed length character string
	varchar	A variable length character string

The data types tinyint, smallint, int & bigint are exactly the same, except for the range of numbers they can store, and the storage requirements. A tinyint takes up 1 byte of storage, and therefore can only store numbers between 0 and 255; a smallint takes up 2 bytes, an int 4 bytes and a bigint 8 bytes. Choose the smallest data type you can get away with. If you need an attribute "week number", a tinyint will suffice; you know up front that there will never be more than 52 weeks in a year.

Handling date and time information is always tricky. Same as with integer data types, there is a smaller alternative to datetime: smalldatetime (that should be easy to remember). Again, this takes up less storage but can store less values; in this case, it stores dates with less precision (up to the second, instead of up to the millisecond).

The data type char stores fixed length text, and you'll have to define what the length is, for example: char(100) will store exactly 100 characters. Quite often, not every record will have the same length for a text field (such as name). In those cases, you can use data type varchar. As with char, you have to define length, but in this case the maximum length; SQL will only store the characters that are actually needed. So storing the text string "false" in a field with data type char(100) will take up 100 bytes; storing the same string in a field with data type varchar(100) will take up 5 bytes, plus a little overhead (SQL uses an additional 2 bytes to store the length). So if you have a text field that will be at most 1 character, don't use an attribute varchar(1) to save storage!

This is all the information on data types we're going to need in this book. Just remember that there are more types available, and that choosing the right type is important.

Nullability

Just like data type, you have to define nullability when you create a table using the GUI. When creating a table using a script, this is optional, but since we'll be using both methods, we'll cover the concept of nullability before we move on to creating a table.

At times, you may not know a value. In the table used as an example above, all fields for all records have a value. But how do you handle the situation where you don't know someone's address, but you still want to store his or her name in the table? One possibility is to insert the string "unknown". But then, if you have a second person without a known address, they would have the same address (at least, according to your data). That may not be what you want.

The solution is to tell SQL that the value is unknown; this is called NULL. At design time, you have to specify whether a NULL value is allowed for this attribute. This is called nullability. For instance, you might decide that "last name" is a mandatory attribute, but "first name" is optional. In that case, you'd define attribute "last name" as NOT NULL, and "FirstName" as NULL.

It is important to know that SQL may not handle unknown values like you'd expect. NULL does not equal NULL, because, using the same address example, just because there are two people whose address you don't know, that doesn't mean they live on the same address; it also does not mean that they don't! The same thing applies when adding values: adding 2 to an unknown number, results in another unknown number. More on this when we start retrieving data from a table; just remember that you may encounter strange results when you allow NULL values, and that you have to test those situations. Now we've handled data types and nullability, let's create a table.

Creating a table

There are two ways to create a table: using the GUI, or with code. We'll start with the easiest way: using the GUI.

Creating a table using the GUI

* Open SSMS, and connect to SQL Server instance;
* Expand **Databases**;
* Expand the test database you've created in chapter 1;
* Expand **Tables** and verify that there is no table called "Persons". If there is, you might be working in the wrong database!
* Right click **Tables** and click **New Table...**;
* Enter "FirstName" for the column name, varchar(100) for the data type and make sure "Allow nulls" is unchecked;
* Do the same for columns "LastName" and "Address";
* On the bottom, there is a tab "Column Properties". You might want to take a look at the available properties, just to give you an idea of the available options;
* Close the screen to create the table. You can do this by right clicking the query window, and choosing "Save Table_1". Enter "Persons" as a name.

Now, the table gets created. However, if you go back to the Object Explorer on the left, it will not show up until you refresh. So right click on tables, and choose Refresh (or hit F5). Now, you'll see your table.

Maybe you've noticed that, in the Object Explorer, the table shows up as "dbo.Persons". In this case, "dbo" is the name of a schema. A schema is a container for tables. The reason for this is security: you can group tables into schemas, and then assign users permission to each schema as needed. For example, you could create two schemas "production" and "sales", put all tables into the relevant schema, and then assign users from the Production department permissions to the production schema (instead of granting permissions on every table individually, which is more work and error prone). This is just one way of assigning permissions (more on that in chapter 6 on permissions).

Schema "dbo" is created automatically whenever you create a database, and we didn't create another schema, so the table "Persons" was put in schema "dbo". By the way: dbo stands for database owner.

If you expand the table "Persons", you can see all the columns you've created. Your table is still empty though.

Creating a table using code

Now, let's create the same table using a script. Right click the table and choose *Script Table as > CREATE To > New Query Editor Window*. A new query window will open, with the required code to create a table. This will look something like this:

```
-- create table dbo.Persons, scripted by SSMS
USE [testdatabase]
GO

/****** Object: Table [dbo].[Persons] Script Date: 01/02/2013 20:37:06 ******/
SET ANSI_NULLS ON
GO

SET QUOTED_IDENTIFIER ON
GO

SET ANSI_PADDING ON
GO

CREATE TABLE [dbo].[Persons](
    [Firstname] [varchar](100) NOT NULL,
    [Lastname] [varchar](100) NOT NULL,
    [Address] [varchar](100) NOT NULL
) ON [PRIMARY]

GO

SET ANSI_PADDING OFF
GO
```

SQL adds some lines of code to the script that are optional. You can learn a lot by creating SQL scripts this way, so we'll discuss these optional statements briefly before we run the script.

* The statement USE [testdatabase] tells SQL to run the script in database "testdatabase". If you are already connected to this database, this statement is not necessary.

* SQL runs this script in batches; these batches are separated by the word GO. This is called a "batch delimiter".

* Everything between /* and */ will be ignored by SQL, so you can put your comments here. The same thing applies to everything on a line following "--". Comment will appear in green. If you save a script, remember to put in some comments about what the scripts does.

* Next are three connection settings (SET ... ON). Connection settings are beyond the scope of this book. Later on in the chapter, we'll cover one setting as an example; the other settings can be found in Books Online.

* The square brackets [ ] are put around every object name. This is necessary if you use special names or special characters. An example of a special name is "database"; you

can't call a column "database" without using the square brackets [ ] whenever you refer to this column name. If you'd try, SQL would generate an error:

Msg 156, Level 15, State 1, Line 3
Incorrect syntax near the keyword 'database'.

* An example of a special character is the space. Try changing "Firstname" to "First name" with and without the square brackets, and notice the differences. We don't recommend using spaces in an object name, or for that matter, any name that requires the square brackets.
* The last optional statement is ON [PRIMARY]. By default, a database has one data file, which is located in a file group called "primary". You can create other files and/or other file groups; if you want to place the table in another file group than "primary", you have to use the "ON [filegroup]" clause.
So the script SQL Server generated for you will have the same result as this one:

```
CREATE TABLE [dbo].[Persons](
       [Firstname]   [varchar](100) NOT NULL,
       [Lastname]    [varchar](100) NOT NULL,
       [Address]     [varchar](100) NOT NULL
)
```

This is the exact same script, but without specifying a lot of settings we've kept at the default value. Execute this code (you can do this by hitting F5 again, or clicking the button with the red exclamation mark, labeled Execute). This will generate an error:

Msg 2714, Level 16, State 6, Line 2
There is already an object named 'Persons' in the database.

SQL will not allow two objects with the same name in the same database; we should have cleaned it up first. Right click the table in Object Explorer and choose Delete (you'll get a "Delete Object" window, in which you have to confirm this).
You can achieve the same result with the following code:

```
DROP TABLE Persons
```

Now you can execute the CREATE TABLE script without errors. If you refresh the Object Explorer, you can see that the table is created once again.

Constraints
In proper database design, it is important to restrict the values of data that can be put in an attribute. We've already seen one way method of restriction: the data type. By choosing a data type for an attribute, you've restricted the values for that attribute: you can't put text in an integer field, or an invalid date into a date field.
One way to further restrict the possible values for an attribute is the *check constraint*. For example, the following check constraint limits the possible values for date of birth:

```
CREATE TABLE [dbo].[Persons2](
       [Firstname] [varchar](100) NOT NULL,
       [Lastname]   [varchar](100) NOT NULL,
       [Address]    [varchar](100) NULL,
```

```
      [DateOfBirth] date,
      CHECK ([DateOfBirth] between '1900-01-01' and '2100-01-01')
);
```

And to prove this works:

```
INSERT persons2
VALUES ('Albert', 'Einstein', 'Ulm, Germany', '1879-05-14');
```

Msg 547, Level 16, State 0, Line 27
The INSERT statement conflicted with the CHECK constraint
"CK__Persons2__DateOf__534D60F1". The conflict occurred in database
"testdatabase", table "dbo.Persons2", column 'DateOfBirth'.
The statement has been terminated.

Check constraints limit the possibility of erroneous data, by errors or fraud. There are
more ways of restricting the allowed values. One of them, which we'll get to in chapter
3, is the *foreign key*, which restricts the allowed values for a field to values in another
table (for example: orders can only be placed by customers for which there is an entry in
the customer table); other ways of restricting allowed values are triggers and stored
procedures (both covered in chapter 4).
We've now created the table; next, we'll put data into it. But first a little bit about the
code.

Transact-SQL
The code we've used is in a language called Transact-SQL (often abbreviated to T-
SQL). The acronym SQL stands for Structured Query Language. T-SQL is Microsoft's
version of SQL. There is an independent organization called the American National
Standards Institute, or ANSI, that defines the language SQL; T-SQL is a superset of this
standard. That means that, in addition to the standard commands, there are some
commands that are specific to Microsoft SQL Server.
SQL commands can be divided into two categories: Data Definition Language (DDL),
and Data Manipulation Language (DML). DDL is used to create and change objects;
DML is used to manipulate data. Up until now, we've used DDL to create (and drop) the
table; in the next paragraph we'll start using DML: the commands INSERT, SELECT,
UPDATE and DELETE.

Insert
At this point, the table is still empty. We'll have to insert some data. To do this, you can
execute the following code:

```
INSERT Persons (Firstname, Lastname, Address)
VALUES ('John', 'Smith', 'First Street 1, Washington');
```

This inserts one record into the table. If you insert data into every field, as we do here,
the list of columns is optional; SQL will put the first value in the first column, and so on.
So the line of code above is the same as the following:

```
INSERT Persons
VALUES ('John', 'Smith', 'First Street 1, Washington');
```

Optionally, you can use "INSERT INTO" instead of "INSERT".

If you only want to insert data into some fields, but not into other fields, you only list the fields you want to use. The other fields should either be nullable, or have a default value. We could have specified a default value for a column when we created the table, like this:

```
CREATE TABLE [Persons] (
        Firstname varchar(100),
        Lastname varchar(100,
        Address varchar(100) NOT NULL
        DEFAULT '1600 Pennsylvania Avenue, Washington D.C.')
```

But we didn't specify a default, and the column does not allow nulls, so we have to give a value for every column. If you do have nullable columns, you can explicitly insert a null value if you want to:

```
INSERT Persons VALUES ('Elvis', 'Presley', NULL);
```

By the way: the semicolon at the end is optional for Microsoft SQL Server in almost every situation, but this will likely change in a future version. So it is probably best to learn it the new way.

Now, insert three more records:

```
INSERT Persons
VALUES ('Peter', 'Jones', 'Second Street 2, London');
INSERT Persons
VALUES ('Frank', 'James', 'Champs-Elysees , Paris');
INSERT Persons
VALUES ('Jim', 'Gray', 'Main Street 7, New York');
```

As an alternative, you can insert all three records with just one statement:

```
INSERT Persons VALUES
('Peter', 'Jones', 'Second Street 2, London')
,('Frank', 'James', 'Champs-Elysees , Paris')
,('Jim', 'Gray', 'Main Street 7, New York');
```

Now we have data in our table; the next step is to retrieve it.

Select

This is where things get more interesting. We'll demonstrate a number of ways to influence what data is returned (called the result set). Just follow along; you'll see how to get all data out of a table, how to get a selection of the data, how to order the data and how to present the data in a different way from how it is stored.

The easiest way is to retrieve everything just the way it is:

```
SELECT          *
FROM    Persons;
```

The asterisk means: return all columns. This, however, is not recommended. You should only retrieve the columns you need. Even if you need all columns, specify them. If, later on, someone adds a column to the table, your statement will still return only the columns needed, and not this extra column. So use this instead:

```
SELECT  Firstname
        ,Lastname
        ,Address
FROM    Persons;
```

For readability, we'll stick to using SELECT * in most examples in this book. Also for readability, the statement is broken up into several lines. There are endless discussions on the internet about how to format SQL code, and you can even buy tools to format the code for you. Readability makes code maintenance and code changes easier, even if you wrote the code yourself. The formatting doesn't matter to SQL Server, though; you could put the entire statement on a single line:

```
SELECT  Firstname, Lastname,Address FROM Persons;
```

In the three statements above, SQL Server will give you every record in whatever order is most convenient for SQL Server. Most likely you'll want to have some control over the sorting of the output. This can be done using ORDER BY:

```
SELECT  *
FROM            Persons
ORDER BY        Lastname;
```

Now, Gray will appear on top, and Smith at the bottom. You can sort by one or more columns:

```
SELECT  *
FROM            Persons
ORDER BY        Lastname, Firstname;
```

In our example, this doesn't matter; this would only matter when two records have the same Lastname. If you want, you can also sort in the opposite direction, using DESC (short for: descending):

```
SELECT  *
FROM            Persons
ORDER BY        Lastname DESC;
```

Now, Smith is on top. The default is to sort ascending ("ASC"), from smallest to largest value.
Instead of returning all rows, you can also filter which rows to return:

```
SELECT  *
FROM            Persons
WHERE   Lastname = 'Jones';
```

This will only return the persons whose last name is Jones; in this case, one record. The WHERE clause is called a constraint. You can also combine filter conditions:

```
SELECT *
FROM    Persons
WHERE   Lastname = 'James'
        or Lastname = 'Jones';
```

An alternative way of writing this is using the keyword IN:

```
SELECT *
FROM    Persons
WHERE   Lastname IN ('James', 'Jones');
```

Some developers find it easier to return all columns and/or all rows, and filter at the client application. Don't fall into this trap; it puts a lot of unnecessary strain on your database server and network.

What if you don't know the exact value you're looking for, but just part of that value? For this, you can use the keyword LIKE, in combination with a wildcard. In T-SQL, there are several wildcards. The most important ones are the % and the underscore (_). You can use a wildcard at the start, the end or anywhere in between. The following query will find every record with a last name starting with the letters "Jam":

```
SELECT *
FROM    Persons
WHERE   Lastname LIKE 'Jam%';
```

There are a lot of ways to filter which records you get back. We'll cover some of those later on. For now, we'll mention just four more:

```
SELECT *
FROM    Persons
WHERE   Lastname IS NULL;
```

This will return all records where "Lastname" is null. If you look at the table create statement, you can see that this query can't possibly return any records, because the attribute Lastname has been defined as "not null". In fact, this is the way SQL Server solves this particular query. It will not even check the actual table; just from the table definition it will know that no records match the filter constraint, and return only the column headers. The same thing happens when you define a filter that is impossible:

```
SELECT *
FROM    Persons
WHERE   Lastname = 'James'
        and Lastname = 'Jones';
```

A last name cannot be both "James" and "Jones". SQL knows this, and returns zero rows without accessing the table.

Another way to filter the records is using the keyword "top". This way, you can limit the amount of records:

```
SELECT TOP 2 *
FROM    Persons;
```

This will only return 2 rows. The keyword "TOP" is often combined with "ORDER BY", as without an "ORDER BY", you can't determine what will be the top records. See for yourself what happens when you order this list by last name, both ascending and descending. This can be quite useful if you need a sample from the data.

At times, there are duplicate values in a row, and you want to filter out the duplicates. That can be done using the keyword "DISTINCT". If you want all last names, but without duplicates, that can be achieved with the following query:

```
SELECT DISTINCT [Lastname]
FROM    Persons;
```

We've now seen how to retrieve some or all columns, and how to retrieve some or all rows. The last thing we want to show you before we start changing the data in the table, is how to change the data as it is returned in the result set (without affecting the data in the table).

First off, we'll start by changing the column headers:

```
SELECT 'Achternaam' = Lastname
FROM    Persons
```

If you don't speak Dutch, the column header probably doesn't make much sense to you, but the code should be obvious anyway. You can use the column alias with or without the single quotes. Often there are several ways to achieve the same result in T-SQL:

```
SELECT Lastname AS 'Achternaam'
FROM    Persons
```

Another way is to change the data in the result set.

```
SELECT    Lastname + ', ' + Firstname AS 'Name'
FROM      Persons;
```

This concatenates Firstname and Lastname. For this to work, every value needs to be non-null. As we mentioned earlier, adding something to an unknown value results in an unknown value; by default, this is also true for text strings. Try this for yourself: insert an additional record with NULL as first name, and rerun this query; the result for this record will be NULL. This may not be what you want, but you can change this. Remember connection settings? We mentioned these while discussing the code that SQL generated to create a table. You can use connection settings to override the default behavior:

```
SET CONCAT_NULL_YIELDS_NULL OFF
```

This way, SQL will treat the unknown text value as an empty string. There is a better way of doing this, as we'll see in the exercises, so we'll clean up our change and turn this setting back to default:

```
SET CONCAT_NULL_YIELDS_NULL ON
```

These examples demonstrate that the data in the result set does not have to be the same as the data in the table. In fact, you can change the data in the result set to any string you like:

```
SELECT 'any string'
FROM    Persons
```

This will return 'any string' once for every record in the table (without affecting the actual table). Not something you'll do quite often, though. There are a lot more functions beside string concatenation that you can use in the SELECT or WHERE clause. We'll cover some of them in the remainder of this book.

We've now seen how to change the data in the result set; next, we'll see how to change the data in the actual table, using UPDATE and DELETE.

Update

You can change a field using the UPDATE clause:

```
UPDATE Persons
SET          Firstname = 'Frank jr.'
WHERE   Firstname = 'Frank';
```

The WHERE clause is very important here. Note that the UPDATE statement updates every record that meets the criteria in the WHERE clause. If you forget to specify a WHERE clause, you'll update every single record in the entire table. Hopefully when this happens to you, you'll have read the chapter about backups and restores.

You can easily check which records will be affected by trying out the WHERE clause in a SELECT statement.

You can also change several fields at once:

```
UPDATE Persons
SET     Firstname = 'Frank'
        , Address = 'Unter den Linden, Berlin'
WHERE   Firstname = 'Frank jr.';
```

Delete

Deleting data is easy.

```
DELETE
FROM    Persons
WHERE   Lastname = 'James';
```

You always delete an entire record, not a single field in a record. Therefore, you don't have to specify the fields you want to delete. The following query doesn't make sense, and results in a syntax error:

```
DELETE *
FROM    Persons
WHERE   Lastname = 'James'
```

As with the update clause, you have to make sure you filter the right record(s) to delete. A delete without a "WHERE" clause will delete every record from the table!

A special situation can occur when you have two records that are exact duplicates. Imagine the situation where you've accidentally inserted the same record twice, and want to undo this by deleting one of the two records. You can achieve this with the following code:

```
DELETE TOP (1)
FROM    Persons
WHERE   Firstname = 'John';
```

With proper database design, this shouldn't happen though; you should make sure that each record can be uniquely identified. More on this in chapter 3, when we talk about primary keys and normalization.

This concludes our first tour of the table.

Summary

In this chapter, we've talked about the central component of the database: the table. A table is made up of rows and columns. A table contains structured data, and the structure for every column has to be designed up front. Two design decisions are the data type and nullability. Other decisions are the name and the data type of the column.

Tables are created using the SSMS GUI, or Transact-SQL code. There are two types of Transact-SQL code: Data Definition Language, and Data Manipulation Language. Data Manipulation is done through SELECT, INSERT, UPDATE and DELETE statements. Result sets can be filtered using the WHERE clause. Other DML keywords are TOP, IN and ORDER BY.

Along the way, we've seen some important design principles:
* Always clean up your mess after you're done (in this case: your database objects);
* Try to choose the smallest data types possible;
* If you save a script, remember to put in some comments about what the script does;
* Format your code for readability;
* Don't use SELECT * in production.

Suggested exercises
* Create a table with all non-nullable columns and see what happens when you try to insert a null value into a column.
* Try to insert more values than columns.
* See if you can use the ISNULL keyword instead of "concat null yields null" to produce the same result as in the example where we concatenated firstname and lastname. You'll probably have to look up the syntax for ISNULL in Books Online for this.

See if you can answer the questions you wrote down at the start of this chapter. If not, look them up in Books Online or on the web, using your favorite search engine.

Questions
This section contains the correct answers to the questions, plus an explanation of the wrong answers. In addition to the correct answers, we'll also give a few pointers which are useful on the actual exam.

QUESTION 1
Which of the following data types would be the most appropriate to store a telephone number?

A Int
B Char (50)
C Varchar (50)
D Bigint
E Varchar

QUESTION 2
Which of the following data types would be most appropriate to store a birthday?

A Datetime
B Smalldatetime
C Date
D Time
E Smalldate

QUESTION 3
A null value is best described as:

A Zero
B Nothing
C Not Known
D None of the above

QUESTION 4
You have a table with all your products. Your company has designed a new product, and the database needs to be updated to include this product. Which statement do you need for this?

A ADD
B UPDATE
C INSERT
D ENTER

QUESTION 5
Which syntax is correct?

A Insert table countries (countrycode = SW, country is Sweden)
B Insert into table countries (countrycode = SW, country = Sweden)
C Insert INTO countries (countrycode, country) VALUES ('SW', 'Sweden')
E All of the above

QUESTION 6

Which statement would retrieve all product names in categories smartphone and tablet?

A SELECT * FROM products WHERE category in ('smartphone', 'tablet')
B SELECT productname FROM products WHERE category = 'smartphone' OR category ='tablet'
C SELECT productname FROM products WHERE category = 'smartphone' AND category ='tablet'
D SELECT * FROM products WHERE category = 'smartphone' UNION SELECT * FROM products WHERE category ='tablet'

QUESTION 7
Given a table with country names, which statement would change the name of the capital of Italy from Roma to Rome?

A UPDATE countries SET capital = 'Rome"
B UPDATE countries SET capital = 'Rome' WHERE country = 'Italy'
C ALTER countries SET capital = 'Rome'
D ALTER countries SET capital = 'Rome' WHERE country = 'Italy'

QUESTION 8
What would be the result of the following query:

DELETE orderdate. FROM orders Where order_number = 17

A The record(s) with order_number 17 would be deleted.
B No records would be deleted.
C The value orderdate for record order_number would be set to NULL.
D Syntax error

QUESTION 9
You find that your order table contains two columns for order date: orderdate and order_date. Which (partial) statement would you use to get rid of the column order_date?

A DROP COLUMN
B DELETE COLUMN
C REMOVE COLUMN
D None of the above. You have to recreate the table.

QUESTION 10
What is an example of DDL?

A Adding a record to a table
B Changing the data type of a column
C Changing the value of an attribute for a single record
D Changing the value of an attribute for every record in a table

Answers

QUESTION 1
The most appropriate answer is C: varchar(50). A telephone number is not a number you would perform calculations on, so the numeric types (*int* and *bigint*) would not be appropriate.
A *varchar(8)* would only fit 8 digits, so this would not be big enough to store a telephone number (though this might depend on the country you live in).
This only leaves *char(50)* and *varchar(50)*. Both would get the job done, but since telephone numbers are less than 50 characters, using *varchar(50)* will reduce storage needs significantly, making this the correct answer.
Notice that the question states: "most appropriate", not "best possible". This means that there might be a better answer; you have to choose the best of the answers provided.

QUESTION 2
If you only need to store a date, the correct data type is: date (answer C). In SQL 2005 and earlier, the *date* data type was not available, therefore you needed to use datetime, so a birthday would be stored as '1971-09-03 00:00:00'.
All data types that store time are too big, and therefore not most appropriate (even though both datetime and smalldatetime would also get the job done).
There is no data type *smalldate*. Microsoft exams often have trick answers like this one. Just remember that, if you're well prepared, and you've never heard of a feature, it is probably not the correct answer.

QUESTION 3
The correct answer is C: not known (as explained in the section on nullability).

QUESTION 4
The correct answer is C: INSERT.
ADD is used in Data Definition Language (DDL), not Data Modification Language (DML). UPDATE is used to change existing records. ENTER is not a T-SQL command.

QUESTION 5
The correct answer is C. Answers A and B do not provide the necessary keyword VALUES. The use of TABLE in answer D is incorrect.
Both the use of the semicolon at the end of the statement and the use of the keyword INTO are optional.

QUESTION 6
The correct answer is B. Answers A and D retrieve all attributes, not just the product name. Answer C will return zero records, since a category cannot be both 'smartphone' and 'tablet'.
And no, there is not, and should not be, a category 'phablet'.

QUESTION 7
The correct answer is B.
Answers A and C lack a WHERE clause, so these statements would update the capital of Italy, and every other capital as well. Though this is not explicitly stated, we must assume that that is not exactly the intended behavior. And just to reiterate: performing an UPDATE without a WHERE clause is a mistake that is easily made in real life, so be careful when updating data.

Answers C and D use the keyword ALTER, which is used in DDL, not DML.

QUESTION 8
The correct answer is D: syntax error. The delete statement deletes entire records, not attributes of a record. Therefore, it doesn't make sense to specify the attribute; the T-SQL syntax reflects this logic.

QUESTION 9
The correct answer is A: DROP COLUMN. DELETE is used in DML, not DDL. REMOVE is not a T-SQL keyword.

QUESTION 10
The correct answer is B: changing the data type of a column. DDL stands for Data Definition Language, and this is the only statement that changes the definition of the table. All the other statements change the actual data in the table, and these are therefore DML statements (Data Manipulation Language).

Chapter 3: Using multiple tables

Chapter overview

In the previous chapters, we've created a database with a single table in it, and learned how to manipulate both the table itself and the data in it. In this chapter, we'll learn how to manipulate multiple tables, and learn about the relation between tables.

Preview
In the previous chapters, we've made a test database and put a table in it with some data. However, a relational database is called relational for a reason. Almost every database will have more than a single table, and the relationships between those tables are important. We'll start this chapter by explaining why you would want to make more tables, and how to do so at the logical level, by a process called normalization. Then we'll show the T-SQL code to create the relationships between the tables.
Once we have multiple tables, we can explore how to perform data manipulation on multiple tables at once.

Key concepts
normalization, first/second/third normal form, primary key, foreign key, UNION, INTERSECT, JOIN

Requirements
You need access to a test database with database owner (dbo) privileges (e.g. the one we created in chapter 1).

Exam objectives
For the exam, the relevant objectives are:
* Understanding what a relational database is, the need for relational database management systems (RDBMS), and how relations are established
* Understand normalization: the reasons for normalization, the five most common levels of normalization, how to normalize a database to third normal form
* Understand primary, foreign, and composite keys
* Understanding the reason for keys in a database, choosing appropriate primary keys, selecting appropriate data type for keys, selecting appropriate fields for composite keys, understanding the relationship between foreign and primary keys
* Extracting data by using joins; combining result sets by using UNION and INTERSECT
* Deleting data from single or multiple tables
* Ensuring data and referential integrity by using transactions

Practice questions
Think of a real life example you'd like to make a database design for. In this chapter, we'll use book sales, so think of another one. Your record collection, sport team results, whatever. Take some time to write down the attributes you'd like to record. Then, based on what you've learnt in the previous chapter, design the tables (on paper) and put some data rows in them.
Write down your own questions.

Database design stages

The process of designing a database is divided into several stages. Not every design project requires a strict division into several phases; smaller projects might use a hybrid approach, whereas large projects might require a strict separation between the phases, with a formal approval at the end of each stage.

The first stage is *requirements gathering*. In this stage, a detailed analysis of the requirements is performed. This can be done by interviewing key personal, reviewing documentation, analyzing current information flow etc.

The second stage is the *conceptual database design*. The requirements from the previous stage are translated into entities, attributes and relations, in an Entity-Relational (ER) model.

The third stage is *logical database design*. In this stage, a process called normalization is used to map the ER model to database tables.

The final stage is *physical database design*. This stage covers aspect such as:
* the layout of files on the Operating System;
* choosing the right data types;
* adding indexes to increase performance.

In the physical database design stage, you design the database specifically for the RDBMS you're going to use (i.e., Oracle, SQL Server, DB2 etc.); all other stages are identical regardless of which database product you're going to use.

In this book, we'll discuss the logical and physical design stages, starting with normalization.

Normalization

In 1970, a computer scientist named Edgar F. Codd formulated the relational database theory. Since then, a lot of books have been written with complex definitions, the details of which (fortunately) are beyond the scope of this book and the exam. It is important to know, however, that a relational database is not something Microsoft has thought up out of the blue. What we'll give you here is a simplified version, but even so, for the exam you'll need to know a bit about the theory of normalization, and be able to apply it. But first, in global terms, the reason for normalization.

What normalization boils down to, is deciding which tables to design, and consequently what data to put in which table. Data should be stored once, and only once. The rules of normalization are meant to avoid situations where you store data more than once, and situations where you can't store the data at all.

Before we dive into the rules for normalization, we'll demonstrate what problems occur when you do not follow these rules. For example, let's look at the following table:

First name	Last name	Address	Item	Quantity	Price
John	Smith	First Street 1, Washington	A Brief History of Time – S. Hawking	1	9.99
Peter	Jones	Second Street 2, London	The Prince – Macchiavelli	10	59.9
Frank	James	Champs-Elysees , Paris	Lord of the Rings – J.R.R. Tolkien	2	17.98
Jim	Gray	Main Street 7, New York	The Prince – Macchiavelli	1	5.99

This is basically the Person table from chapter 2, but we've expanded it to store sales data for a book store; the book purchase is now added to the table. Each record now represents a single order, so we'll call the table "Orders". You'd expect an "Order date" in this table, but we won't be needing this for our example.

Now what happens when you discover "Machiavelli" has been misspelled? You have to update 2 records. Not much work in a small table such as this, but something you definitely want to avoid in larger tables. Not only is it more work to update two records instead of one, you also run the risk of updating only one record, not both, if something goes wrong. Bottom line: storing data only once is part of proper database design.

A second issue occurs when you want to delete a purchase record (maybe the order was cancelled). Now, you have no place left to store the address for the customer. This is something your marketing department won't be pleased about.

A third issue is the possibility of a person buying two books. To allow a second item, for even one record, the table's design would have to be expanded with three extra columns (item, quantity & price). Even without the Address column, the resulting table hardly fits on the page, but you get the idea of adding columns.

First name	Last name	Item#1	Q#1	Price#1	Item#2	Q#2
John	Smith	A Brief History of Time – S. Hawking	1	9.99	The Prince – Macchiavelli	1
Peter	Jones	The Prince – Macchiavelli	10	59.9		
Frank	James	Lord of the Rings – J.R.R. Tolkien	2	17.99		
Jim	Gray	The Prince – Macchiavelli	1	5.99		

And again for a third, a fourth etc. That would mean storing a lot of empty attributes: Peter didn't buy a second book, so the attributes Item#2 and Q#2 are empty for the record of his purchase. It also means unnecessarily difficult queries. For example, to find out who ordered more than a single copy of a book, the query would become:

```
SELECT [First Name]
      ,[Last Name]
FROM   Orders
WHERE  (Item#1 = 'book title' AND Q#1 > 1)
    OR (Item#2 = 'book title' AND Q#2 > 1);
```

And because the table design would have to be changed again if a third set of columns was added, so would this query; a very inflexible design. These are the sort of problems normalization is meant to prevent: storing redundant data, inability to store data and inflexible database design. Now let's look at how normalization solves those problems.

Normal Forms

Normalization follows a set of rules. If your table adheres to only the first rule, it is said to be in First Normal Form, or 1NF. If it adheres to the second rule, but not the third, it is said to be in Second Normal Form, or 2NF, etc. A table in a certain level of normalization automatically adheres to the lower levels, so a table in 2NF by definition adheres to the rules of 1NF. The highest level is 5NF. A database has a certain level if every table in the database has that level, or higher.

The table above doesn't follow any normalization rules. We'll use this table to clarify the five levels of normalization. To make it easier to read, we'll just use the table description (without the data):

Orders
- [First name]
- [Last name]
- Address
- [Item #1]
- [Quantity #1]
- [Price #1]
- [Item #2]
- [Quantity #2]
- [Price #2]

By the way: this diagram is created in SSMS. To create such a diagram: under Databases, expand your database and right click on Database Diagrams; just add the tables you need. Pay attention, however, that when you change something in the diagram, you might be changing the actual tables. Creating diagrams this way is helpful when documenting a database design.

First Normal Form

A database in first normal form must:
* Have a primary key (that is, a column or set of columns that uniquely identifies each record);
* Eliminate repeating groups.

Memorize these rules for the exam. The first step is determining a primary key, so we'll have to look for an attribute or combination of attributes that can uniquely identify each row. Such an attribute (or combination of attributes) is called a candidate key. A candidate key is therefore a candidate to be designated as the primary key. A table might have multiple candidate keys; in our table, we do not have such an attribute, so we'll have to add one.

By the way: for a combination of attributes to be considered a candidate key, it has to be the *smallest* possible subset of attributes to uniquely identify a row. For example: if SSN uniquely identifies a row, obviously every combination of that attribute and another attribute would also uniquely identify a row, but no such combination would be considered a candidate key.

First, we'll add the primary key. To do this, we add a column called "OrderID", and designate this as a primary key. In it, we'll store an order number. A primary key value has to be unique; therefore, the column cannot be NULL (since a NULL value is unknown, two NULL values may or may not be the same).

In the Database Diagram, the Primary key is represented by the golden key icon.

Now, we can uniquely identify each row by order number; the first requirement for 1NF. Now the second requirement: no repeating groups.

Our example has a repeating group of attributes: item, quantity and price are stored twice. And if you'd want to add a third item, even for a single customer, you'd have to add three additional columns. As mentioned, this repeating grouping of columns causes lots of empty fields, and may cause table and query redesign.

There is another form of repeatable grouping of attributes, where multiple pieces of data are stored in the same columns (instead of in different columns). An example would be an "Author" attribute in a "Books" table. Some books have multiple authors, in which case you could design a table with just a single author attribute, and store all authors in that single attribute, for example as a comma separated list: "author 1, author 2, author 3". It is sometimes argued that this form of repeatable grouping doesn't violate the 1NF rule, but you probably shouldn't do it anyway; a more elegant solution is shown further on.

So, to eliminate the repeating groups in our example table, we have to split our order into order lines:

The table "orders" now has a composite primary key; each row can be uniquely identified by the combination of order number and order line number. Here you can see that in a composite primary key, it is not the value of a single column but rather the combination of values that has to be unique. For example: if the order with OrderID 17 would consist of 4 different items, your table would have 4 records with OrderID 17, but each record would have a different order line number. Along the same lines, a lot of different orders would have order line number 1, and this wouldn't violate the primary key principle. By the way: a different term for a composite key is a compound key.

Now, we've eliminated the repeated groupings and created the primary key, and in doing so, we've now transformed the unnormalized table into 1NF.

Second Normal Form

A database in second normal form must:
* Follow the rules for 1NF;
* Have attributes that are depended on the whole primary key (fully functionally dependent), not just on a part of the composite key.

In our Orders table, "customer" is related to an order (and therefore OrderID), not to the composite key OrderID + Line Item Number. This is because you can't have an order line for customer A and an order line for customer B on the same order; all order lines on a single order are related to the same customer. So we have to split the table to put Customer + OrderID information in one table, and OrderID + Order Line Number (plus related attributes) in the other:

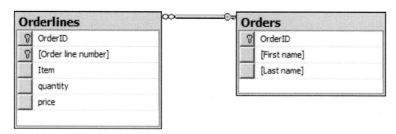

This eliminates some repeating data, since now, customer information doesn't have to be stored for each Order line item. Also, each attribute in the OrderLines table is now said to be fully functionally dependent on the composite key "OrderID & Order line number".

We've now created a relationship between the two tables (linked by way of the OrderID). In the diagram, this is represented by the line between the two tables, with the key on the one side, and an infinity symbol on the other side. By the way: the column OrderId in the OrderLines table, the one that points to the corresponding record in the "Orders" table, is called a foreign key, because it points to a foreign table.

A foreign key does not necessarily have to reference the primary key of the other table; it can reference any column, as long as the values in this column are unique. This makes perfect sense: if a foreign key references OrderID, and two OrdersID would match, how can SQL know which one is needed? It can't, so the value in the referenced column has to be unique. Moreover, it has to be *enforced* as unique, either as a primary key or by adding the keyword "UNIQUE":

```
CREATE TABLE test1 (
       column1     int
     , column2     int    UNIQUE
     , PRIMARY KEY (column1));
```

A foreign key can be defined on a NULL column (meaning every value has to be either NULL or present in the foreign table), but it can't reference a NULL column.

We'll talk more about foreign keys and how to create them in a few pages, but for now, back to our order tables. One order can have many line items, but a line item always belongs to a single order. Therefore, the relation between the tables "Orders" and "OrderLines" is called a one-to-many relation (1:N). There are two other types of relations: one-to-one relation (1:1) and many-to-many (N:M, not N:N as this would imply the same number of records on both sides). The many-to-many relation is implemented by way of a 1:M, a 1:N and a table in between (called a link table or junction table). To stay with the book example: an author may write many books, and a book may have many authors. The table design would look like this:

For a book with id 1 by three authors, with id 4, 5, & 6, the junction table "Bookauthors" would have three records: (1, 4), (1, 5) and (1, 6). This is a more elegant solution than storing all authors in a single attribute.

We've now made all attributes dependent on the primary key of its table, turning our example database into 2NF.

Third Normal Form

A database in third normal form must:
* Follow the rules for 2NF;
* Eliminate attributes that are not (directly) dependent on the key (and move them to a separate table).

In our example, "First name", "Last Name" and "Address" do not depend on primary key OrderID, but on an entity "customer". So we have to split the table "Orders" into two tables: a smaller table "Orders" and a new table "Customers". We don't have to change table "OrderLines".

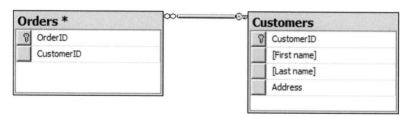

Again, we have to link the two tables. We create a primary key for the new table "Customers" and replace the 3 attributes for customer in the "Orders" table with that newly created primary key; next, we create a foreign key on "CustomerID" in the "Orders" table to point to "CustomerID", the primary key in the "Customers" table.

As stated, a primary key is a column or combination of columns that uniquely identifies each record. The combination of first name and last name is unique with our limited set of customers, but we can't rely on this. Adding a Social Security Number to the table would fix this; so would adding a unique number. SQL has the option of generating a unique number for each row, called an identity column. Some people prefer to use an externally generated number (like SSN), others prefer to create their own. Let's choose the latter; we'll add an identity column, called CustomerID. We can do this by specifying the keyword "IDENTITY" in the column definition:

```
1  CREATE TABLE Customers (
2  L     CustomerID int IDENTITY
3        ...
```

Whenever you insert a record into this table, you can't provide a value this identity column; SQL will automatically insert the next number into this column, starting with 1, then 2 etc. If you don't want to start at 1 and increase by 1, you can specify the starting number (seed) and the increment:

```
1  CREATE TABLE Customers (
2  ├     CustomerID int IDENTITY(100,10)
3  L     ...
```

In this example, the Customers will be numbered 100, 110, 120 etc. If you must, you can explicitly insert values into a column marked as an identity column. To do this, you have to enable this feature (and turn it off afterwards):

```
SET IDENTITY_INSERT Customers ON
INSERT Customers VALUES ...
SET IDENTITY_INSERT Customers OFF
```

With this identity column, each record in the "Customers" table can be uniquely identified by "CustomerID".

One final detail about the primary key. In chapter 2 we talked about data types, and said that it is important to choose the smallest possible data type (but one that would still allow you to store all possible values). This is even more important in the case of a primary key, as this is often referenced by a foreign key, and as such, stored in more than one table. In Chapter 5, we'll talk about indexes, and there we'll see that a primary key is often used as clustered index; in that case, the primary key is stored in every nonclustered index as well, making selecting the smallest data type all the more important.

We've now made sure that every attribute in the table directly depends upon the primary key, thus making it 3NF. We won't go to 4NF or 5NF.

Real world usage

In the real world, normalization is very useful, but it has its limitations. In the example used above, "customer" is moved to a separate table, but "address" is not. This may or may not make sense in your situation. The idea behind normalization is to put separate entities in separate tables, and a customer is definitely something else than an order. But technically, so is an "address". Two people can share the same address, and one person can have several addresses: a shipping address, a billing address, a vacation address and maybe even a history of every former address. Does your database really need to store an unknown amount of addresses per person? If so, use separate tables; if not, don't. Normalizing a database makes it harder to retrieve data, because you need to join several tables to get all the data you want. Queries will be harder to write, and performance might suffer (depending on the type of queries). Most often, normalizing a database to 3NF will be sufficient (this might be the reason why the exam objective requires that you know "how to normalize a database to third normal form", not fifth normal form). Use 3rd normal form as your starting point; from there on, adjust if necessary. Do not dogmatically follow the normalization rules to the letter. Learn the theory, and then think about what makes sense in your situation.

T-sql table relations

DDL: Creating table relations

In the preceding part, we've seen how to design the right tables, and link these tables using primary and foreign keys. Now, we'll look at the Data Definition Language, the T-SQL code to create these keys.

Primary key

To create the primary key for the Customers table, just add "PRIMARY KEY" in the column definition:

```
1  CREATE TABLE Customers (
2       CustomerID int IDENTITY PRIMARY KEY
3       ,[First name] varchar(100)
4       ,[Last name] varchar(100)
5       ,[Address] varchar(100));
```

As an alternative, you can specify the primary key separately, as you can see in line 6 of the following code:

```
1  CREATE TABLE Customers (
2       CustomerID int IDENTITY
3       ,[First name] varchar(100)
4       ,[Last name] varchar(100)
5       ,[Address] varchar(100)
6       ,PRIMARY KEY (CustomerID));
```

In the case of a composite primary key, you have to use the second method. Put all the columns of the composite primary key between the parentheses, separated by commas. As a test, try inserting two records into the table with the same CustomerID, and see what happens.

Foreign key

To create a foreign key, use the keyword "REFERENCES" , followed by the table name and (in parentheses) the column that is referenced:

```
1  CREATE TABLE Orders (
2       OrderID int PRIMARY KEY
3       ,CustomerID int NULL
4       REFERENCES Customers(CustomerID));
```

As stated, the foreign key has to reference a column whose values are unique; more specifically, a column whose values are enforced by SQL to be unique. This column can be either a primary key or a column that has been defined with a unique constraint. We've already seen how to create a unique constraint:

```
1  CREATE TABLE Test1 (
2      column1     int
3      ,column2    int     UNIQUE
4      ,PRIMARY KEY (column1));
```

Obviously, the table being referenced by the foreign key has to exist before you can create the foreign key. Otherwise, SQL will generate an error:

Msg 1767, Level 16, State 0, Line 1
Foreign key 'FK__Orders__Customer__286302EC' references invalid table 'Customers'.
Msg 1750, Level 16, State 0, Line 1
Could not create constraint. See previous errors.

Dropping the tables has to be done in the opposite order, the table with the foreign key before the table being referenced. This is an example where you can see that SQL actually enforces the relationship. If you were able to drop the wrong table first, the foreign key would point to a non-existing table. Another example is when you insert a value into a column with a foreign key; SQL will only allow the insert if the value actually exists in the table being referenced. Otherwise, it will generate an error:

Msg 547, Level 16, State 0, Line 2
The INSERT statement conflicted with the FOREIGN KEY constraint
"FK__Orders__Customer__3A81B327". The conflict occurred in database
"testdatabase", table "dbo.Customers", column 'CustomerID'.
The statement has been terminated.

In this case, this means you can't create a sales order for a customer that doesn't exist. And again, this also works the other way around. If you try to delete a record that is being referenced by a foreign key, this will also be prevented by SQL: you can't delete customer information without first deleting the order records for that customer.
This is called *referential integrity*: SQL Server ensures that no record in a child table can exist without a corresponding record in parent table. Referential integrity is one of the cornerstones of the relational database model.
By the way: did you notice the name of the foreign key in both error messages? SQL Server automatically generated this name when it created the table "Orders". Not very nice, or descriptive. A better way is to supply the name yourself. Instead of defining the constraint along with the column, you define the constraint explicitly, like this:

```
CREATE TABLE Orders (
    OrderID int
    ,CustomerID int
    ,CONSTRAINT PK_Orders PRIMARY KEY (OrderID)
    ,CONSTRAINT FK_Orders_Customers FOREIGN KEY (CustomerID)
    REFERENCES Customers(CustomerID));
```

Now, the primary key will be called PK_orders, and the foreign key FK_Orders_customers; this will make an error message easier to decipher.
You can also add a constraint after creating the table, by altering the table definition. Here is how to add a unique constraint for a table that already exists:

```
ALTER TABLE orders
```

```
ADD CONSTRAINT UQ_customer_id UNIQUE (CustomerID);
```

It wouldn't make business sense to add this constraint, because you'd prevent customers from making a second order, but we have to work with the example tables we have; this is the right code to add that nonsensical constraint.
We've now created the tables; now let's start adding data.

DML: Manipulating data for multiple tables

In chapter 2, we've seen how to manipulate data in a single table, using SELECT, INSERT, DELETE and UPDATE statements. Now, we'll look at the differences when querying multiple tables. Keywords like TOP, WHERE and ORDER BY work the same as when querying a single table, so, to keep the examples to the point, we will omit those keywords wherever possible.

Selecting data from multiple tables

Basically, there are four reasons for combining the results of multiple tables:
* when you need different attributes from different tables, basically to undo the effects of normalization. For this, we use the JOIN clause;
* when you need similar attributes, but from different tables. For this, we can use UNION, INTERSECT and EXCEPT;
* when you need to insert or update a table based on data from another table;
* Using subqueries, a very flexible way to do all kinds of cool stuff, but easier demonstrated than explained.

JOIN

We'll start with the first: the join. In our book sales example, we've split our database into 3 tables. To make the next examples more meaningful, we've added a column "OrderDate" to the table "Orders".

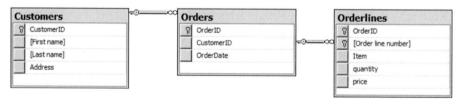

Now consider the following question: when did customer John Smith buy something? To answer that, we need to combine tables "Orders" and "Customers". This is done by joining the tables. The wrong way to do this, is just selecting both tables:

```
SELECT *
FROM    customers, orders
```

This will give a result set of 16 records: each row of customers (4) combined with each row of orders (4). This is called a Cartesian product. Most combinations, however, don't mean anything; the combination of an order date from customer A with the personal details from customer B sounds pretty nonsensical; we only need the rows from the "Orders" table that matches the row from the "Customers" table, i.e. rows that have the same customerID. When using multiple tables, you have to tell SQL which table a particular column is in. The way to do this, is referring to the column with the table name, as in "table.column":

```sql
SELECT *
FROM    Customers, Orders
WHERE   Customers.CustomerID = Orders.CustomerID;
```

This at least gives us the results we want, but we're not there yet. First of all, typing out the full table name gets boring pretty quickly, so we're going to use a table alias. This table alias can be any name you want; a short and practical way is to use the first letter of the table.

```sql
1  SELECT    *
2    FROM      Customers c, Orders o
3  WHERE     c.CustomerID = o.customerID;
```

Still, filtering in the WHERE clause is not the "right" way to join tables. This is the "right" way according to the ANSI standard:

```sql
SELECT *
FROM    Customers c JOIN Orders o ON c.CustomerID = o.CustomerID;
```

The reasoning behind this is to separate the join conditions from the other filtering conditions, making the code easier to read. Some people might say that the ANSI standard is only easier to read once you understand joins, and that for beginners, putting the join columns in the WHERE clause may be easier. However, the result of both queries is the same.

Now, we're getting close; we need to filter the orders from John Smith and select only the right columns:

```sql
SELECT c.[first name]
       ,c.[last name]
       ,o.[orderdate]
FROM    Customers c JOIN Orders o ON c.CustomerID = o.CustomerID
WHERE   c.[first name] = 'John'
        AND c.[last name] = 'Smith';
```

Earlier on we said we would use the asterisk for readability; here, we've replaced the asterisk by the actual columns we need in order to demonstrate the usefulness of the table alias.

The result of the join is to return only those records with a matching value in both tables. This is called an inner join. There is an alternative to that: the outer join. Suppose you want to make a complete list of all customers and the last time they bought something. If you were to use the inner join, you'd only see the customers who bought something, not the customers who never bought anything. If you want to include these customers as well, use the outer join.

There are three types of outer join: right outer join, left outer join and full outer join. All three types of outer join return the records with a match in both tables; the difference between the join types are the additional records that are returned, the ones without a match in both tables:

[64]

* The left outer join (or left join) adds the records from the left table that have no matching record in the right table (with NULL values for the attributes of the right-hand table). If "Customers" is the left-hand table and "Orders" is the right-hand table, and CustomerID the join column, this would mean the customers without an order.
* The right outer join (or right join) as you may guess, does the exact opposite. If "Customers" is the left-hand table and "Orders" is the right-hand table, and CustomerID the join column, this would mean the orders without a customer (not that we should have any, with the correct foreign key).
* The full outer join (or full join) adds both the records from the left-hand table without a match in the right-hand table, as well as the records from the right-hand table without a match in the left-hand table. If "Orders" is the left-hand table and "Customers" is the right-hand table, and CustomerID the join column, this would mean both the orders without a customer, and the customers without an order.

For all records without a match in the other table, NULL values will be returned for the attributes of the other table. To use one of these join types, just replace "JOIN" by the join type you need.
This can be demonstrated by inserting some records, among which a customer without an order and an order without a customer. To allow for records in the "Orders" table without a corresponding record in the "Customer" table, we have to recreate the table without the foreign key.

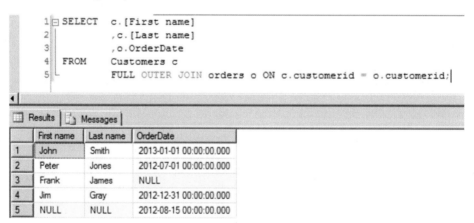

An inner join would return records 1, 2 & 4; a left outer join would return 1, 2, 3 and 4; a right outer join would return 1, 2, 4 and 5.
Joining is not limited to two tables; you can join as many tables as you need. In SQL 2005 there was a limit of 256 tables, but this has been increased for SQL 2008. But if you're joining more than 256 tables, you should seriously consider if you really need this; joining multiple tables, especially large tables, can cause a serious load on the database server. But in case you need to join more than two tables, this is an example of a three table join:

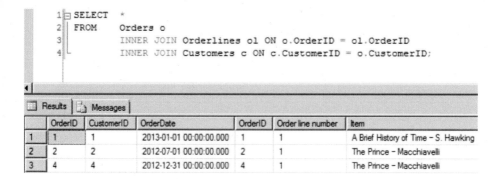

The columns from table "Customers" are included in the result set, just not in the screenshot because otherwise the text would become too small to read.

UNION, INTERSECT and EXCEPT

There will be times when you need to combine similar attributes from different tables (the second reason we mentioned to query multiple tables). Suppose you have a customer table and an employee table, and you need the addresses for a mailing campaign. First, let's set up an employee table:

```
CREATE TABLE Employees (
        EmployeeID int IDENTITY
        ,[First name] varchar(100)
        ,[Last name] varchar(100)
        ,[Address] varchar(100)
        ,PRIMARY KEY (EmployeeID));

INSERT INTO Employees
VALUES ('Barry','St. John','Broadway 5, New York');
INSERT Employees
VALUES ('Jim','Gray','Main Street 7, New York');
```

The following query will give the address of both employees and customers in a single result set:

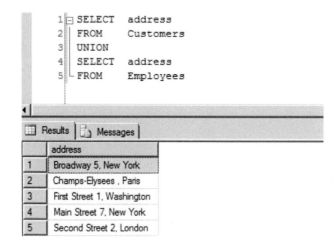

There are some restrictions to the result sets you can join. Both parts of the query will need to select the same number of columns. Technically, the columns do not need to be the same attribute, but the data types need to be compatible; if column X in the first result set has a varchar data type, column X from the second result set can't be a datetime data type. But just to show that the attributes do not have to be the same, you could do the following, because the data types for FirstName and LastName are the same:

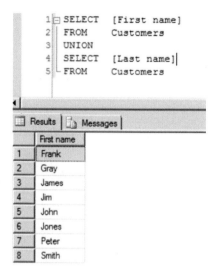

Now, what if one of your employees is also a customer? Won't he appear twice? No. A UNION will only return those records once. You may have noticed Jim Gray is both a customer and an employee. If you didn't notice, this deduplication can easily be demonstrated by using the same select statement twice:

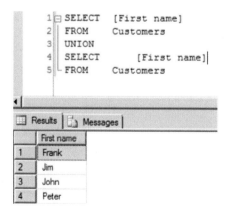

For SQL, this deduplication requires an extra operation; after combining the two result sets, SQL will look for duplicate records, and eliminate those. If you already know that there are no duplicates, or if you don't mind duplicates, you should save SQL the extra work and use "UNION ALL" instead of "UNION". See for yourself what the effect will be om the last statement if you replace "UNION" with "UNION ALL".

Maybe you are just interested in the employees who are also customers. In that case, use "INTERSECT":

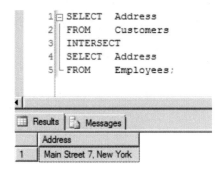

If, for whatever reason, you are only interested in the customers who are not also employees, use "EXCEPT":

In the case of EXCEPT, it matters which table you put first; only records from that table will be returned (minus the records from the second table); in the case of UNION and INTERSECT, it doesn't matter which table you put first.

Updating or inserting from another table
Let's move on to the third reason to combine several tables in a query. If you already have the data in a table, and need to insert this data into another table, there are two methods you can select the data from one table into the other. The first method is when you have already created the target table:

```
INSERT Customers ([First name], [Last name], [Address])
SELECT [First name], [Last name], [Address]
FROM    Employees;
```

The second method is when you haven't created the target table yet. The following statement will create the target table and copy all records from the source table. This is very convenient in testing and development.

```
SELECT *
INTO    Employees_copy
FROM    Employees;
```

For every column you select, The metadata of the column in the new table will be the same as in the old table, i.e. the same name, data type and nullability.

Subqueries

The final way to query multiple tables is the subquery. A subquery is a query, nested in another query. This is why it is also called a nested query. You can use a subquery anywhere a result set is used, for example in the SELECT, FROM and WHERE clause. Let's do this in reverse order, and start with the WHERE clause.

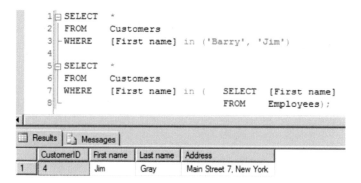

Both queries produce the same result. In the second query, we've used a subquery in the WHERE clause; this is called a predicate subquery. A subquery can be used in the FROM clause as well, in which case it is called a table subquery:

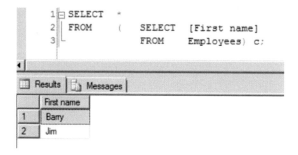

The subquery will create a list of names; the outer query will use this list as if it were a table. Notice the table alias in line 3? When you use the result of a subquery where you'd use a table in the FROM clause, a table alias is required. This example is obviously contrived, as the outer query does nothing to alter the results of the subquery, but it does show the correct way to use a table subquery.

Now, what would be a more realistic example of the use of a subquery in the FROM clause? With the limited amount of tables we have in our example book sales database, it is hard to come up with an example that shows the usefulness of a table subquery. So let's make a new table. Our Customers table has a field "address". Remember that in chapter 2, we said that address would be more than one field in the real world? Now, we'll make a table with address split into several fields.

```
CREATE TABLE Shipments (
        ShipmentID              int identity
        ,Shipmentdate           datetime
        ,[Street name]          varchar(100)
```

```
        , [House number]          varchar(10)
        , [City]                  varchar(100));
```

How would you join this with the "Customers" table? The correct answer would be to
include the CustomerID, but that would defeat the point of this example. We're instead
going to join on Address. To do that, we have to concatenate the address:

```
 1  --subquery
 2  SELECT   'Address' = [Street name] + [House number] + ', ' + City
 3  FROM     Shipments
 4
 5  --outer query
 6  SELECT   *
 7  FROM     Customers c
 8           INNER JOIN (...) s on c.Address = s.Address
 9
10  --Total
11  SELECT   *
12  FROM     Customers c
13           INNER JOIN (SELECT   'Address' = [Street name] + [House number] + ', ' + City
14                       FROM     Shipments
15                      ) s on c.Address = s.Address;
16
```

To make the code easier to read, the screenshot shows the two queries separately; the
subquery has to be placed between the parentheses in the second query; this results in
the third query. This is a good example of when you'd use a table subquery instead of a
table: in cases you don't need the table 'as is', but slightly modified.
A subquery can also be used in the SELECT clause, but only if it returns a single value.
This is called a **scalar** subquery.

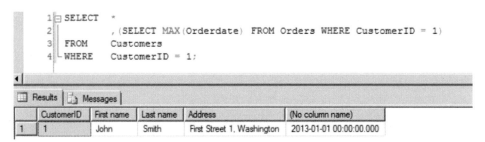

```
 1  SELECT   *
 2           , (SELECT MAX(Orderdate) FROM Orders WHERE CustomerID = 1)
 3  FROM     Customers
 4  WHERE    CustomerID = 1;
```

	CustomerID	First name	Last name	Address	(No column name)
1	1	John	Smith	First Street 1, Washington	2013-01-01 00:00:00.000

We've now seen how to select from multiple tables at once, by using joins and
subqueries. You can't do the same for deletes, inserts & updates; you still have to use
separate statements to do that. But you can combine multiple deletes, inserts & updates
in a transaction (which we'll cover next).
Specifically for foreign key relations, there is a notable exception. When creating a
table, it is possible to specify ON DELETE CASCADE. This will delete the child items
when the parent item is deleted (for example, the orders for a customerID when the
corresponding CustomerID is deleted from the Customer table). A single "delete from
customers where customerid = ..." would cause a "delete from orders where customerid
= ..." . There is also a ON UPDATE CASCADE. Cascading deletes & updates is a bit
too advanced for this book, so we won't go deeper into that.

Transactions
A transaction is a set of actions that have to be performed as a unit: either all actions
have to succeed, or all have to fail. The classic example of this is a bank transaction.

When you transfer money from one account to another, two actions have to be performed: the amount has to be added to one account, and subtracted from the other account. Should the computer crash during the transfer, and only one action be performed, somebody is going to be short of money. Therefore, either all actions have to be completed, or none at all; this transaction is therefore considered to be an atomic unit of work (the word atom comes from ancient Greek, meaning uncuttable or "something that cannot be divided further"; this was before quantum mechanics proved that atoms can indeed be divided further).

There are two types of transactions: explicit and implicit. Every single statement in SQL Server is always executed as a transaction. For example: if you execute an update statement to update two records, either both records get updated, or none. Should the server crash between the first and second update, SQL uses the transaction log to roll back the update of the first record. This is an implicit transaction.

If you want multiple statements to be treated as a single unit of work, you have to use an explicit transaction. This is what an explicit transaction looks like:

```
BEGIN TRANSACTION

        -- action 1
        -- action 2
        -- action 3

COMMIT TRANSACTION;
```

The possibility of hardware failure is one reason to use transactions. If your SQL Server crashes before committing the transaction, all actions performed already per will be rolled back when the database comes back online. You can be certain that all actions that have been performed, will be undone.

There is another situation in which a transaction will be rolled back: if you tell SQL Server to do so. You can check the desired outcome before committing the transaction, and if something is wrong, roll back instead. The next example assumes you know that your last statement affects exactly 1 record. There is a system function that tells you how many records have been affected by the last statement: @@ROWCOUNT. That means you can check how many rows have been affected, and roll back if the value of @@ROWCOUNT is not what you expected (in this case: 1) . In the code below, we'll use this system function. We'll also substitute TRANSACTION for the shorter TRAN.

```
BEGIN TRAN

        -- action 1
        -- action 2
        -- action 3
IF @@ROWCOUNT = 1
COMMIT TRAN
ELSE
ROLLBACK TRAN
```

This example shows a very basic form of error handling. Error handling is very important in real life. We'll see just a little bit more of error handling in chapter 4.

But let's go back to our example. We want to delete a customer and all his orders. As you can see in the screenshot below, if the last delete statement does not delete exactly one record, the first two delete statements will be rolled back.

```
 1 BEGIN TRAN
 2
 3      DELETE
 4      FROM    Orderlines
 5      WHERE   OrderID in (    SELECT  OrderID
 6                              FROM    Orders
 7                              WHERE   CustomerID = 2);
 8
 9      DELETE
10      FROM    Orders
11      WHERE   OrderID in (    SELECT  OrderID
12                              FROM    Orders
13                              WHERE   CustomerID = 2);
14      DELETE
15      FROM    Customers
16      WHERE   CustomerID = 2;
17
18 IF @@ROWCOUNT = 1
19 COMMIT TRAN
20 ELSE
21 ROLLBACK TRAN
```

We've now explained the implicit and explicit transaction, and how transactions can be used for data consistency and error handling.

Summary

In this chapter, we've talked about the way to design tables by a process called normalization. There are 5 successive levels of normalization, First Normal Form (1NF) to Fifth Normal Form (5NF), each with its own rules. The practical summary of these rules is:
* For 1NF, give each table a primary key and eliminate repeating groupings;
* For 2NF, each attribute has to depend on this primary key, and the whole primary key (not just a part of this primary key in case of a composite primary key). Otherwise, move it to a separate table;
* For 3NF, each attribute has to depend directly on this primary key (not through something else). Otherwise, move it to a separate table.

For the exam, you'll have to know the definitions we've given in the main text; you'll probably be tested on these definitions, and how to correctly apply them to real world examples.
A primary key is an attribute, or a combination of attributes, by which you can uniquely identify each record. A foreign key column is a column that references an attribute in another table, either a primary key or a column that has been defined as unique.
There are various ways to select data from multiple tables: JOIN, UNION, INTERSECT and EXCEPT. To update, insert or delete from multiple tables, you need either separate statements, or separate statements combined in a transaction. A transaction is a combination of actions that are either performed as a whole, or rolled back as a whole.

QUESTION 1
Which is not a phase of database design?

A Interviewing users
B Conceptual design
C Logical design
D Physical design

QUESTION 2
Your company has created an application that uses an Oracle database that has to be migrated to SQL server. Which database design phase has to be revised?

A Application design
B Requirements gathering
C Physical design
D Logical design

QUESTION 3
Which line of code contains an error?

```
1  CREATE TABLE [Sales].[Orders] (
2      OrderID     int NULL PRIMARY KEY
3      ,Customer   varchar(100) NULL
4      ,Orderdate  smalldatetime NOT NULL);
```

A Line 1
B Line 2
C Line 3
D Line 4

QUESTION 4
AuthorTitle is a junction table with a composite primary key. The combination AuthorID and TitleID uniquely identifies each row. DatePublished is the date of publication and is functionally dependent on titleID. Priority is the ordinal number of the author in (in the case of multiple authors) with a default of 1, and is functionally dependent on AuthorID and TitleID. Which NF is this?

A 0 NF
B 1 NF
C 2 NF
D 3 NF

QUESTION 5

What is not a good reason to use an explicit transaction?

A Error handling
B grouping multiple statements
C Protecting a single statement against hardware failure

QUESTION 6

What statement is true to regarding the difference between a unique constraint and a primary key constraint?

A These are synonyms
B A foreign key can reference a primary key, but not a unique key
C A primary key allows null values, a unique constraint does not
D A table can have multiple unique constraints, but only one primary key

QUESTION 7

Which T-SQL statement do you use to create a foreign key?

A REFERENCES
B FOREIGN KEY
C Nothing, this can only be done through the SSMS GUI

QUESTION 8

You have loaded two CSV files into a database, into two separate tables. You need to know which records appear in both of the tables. Which keyword should you use?

A UNION
B UNION ALL
C INTERSECT
D EXCEPT

QUESTION 9

You company's database has two tables: Products and Sales. Your manager requires a report, detailing the sales per product. Each product must be included in the report, even products without sales. Which T-SQL keywords do you need for your report?

A LEFT OUTER JOIN
B INNER JOIN
C UNION
D UNION ALL

QUESTION 10

We've added the attributes DateOfBirth and Gender to our [dbo].[Persons] table. In which Normal Form is the resulting table?

- ⊟ 🔲 dbo.Persons
  - ⊟ 📁 Columns
    - 🔳 Firstname (varchar(100), null)
    - 🔳 Lastname (varchar(100), null)
    - 🔳 Address (varchar(100), null)
    - 🔳 DateOfBirth (date, null)
    - 🔳 Gender (char(1), null)

A Not normalized
B 1NF
C 2NF
D 3NF

[76]

Answers

This section contains the correct answers to the questions, plus an explanation of the wrong answers. In addition to the correct answers, we'll also give a few pointers which are useful on the actual exam.

QUESTION 1
The correct answer is A. Interviewing users is not a database design stage, but a part of the requirements gathering phase.

QUESTION 2
The correct answer is C. The database design stages are: Requirements Gathering, Conceptual, Logical, Physical. Of these stages, all but Physical are RDMBS agnostic. Application redesign might also have to be performed, but this answer is incorrect because it is not a database design stage.

Exam tip: notice that questions 1 & 2 cover the same question. At times, the possible answers for a question might cause you to rethink a previous question. In this case, one of the answers to question 2 is "Requirements Gathering"; if you've selected "interviewing key users" as the correct answer for question 1, this might hint you that this is not actually the formal name of the stage. Be careful though: revisiting previous questions can take a long time.

QUESTION 3
The correct answer is line 2. A primary key cannot be defined on a nullable column.

QUESTION 4
The correct answer is B, 1st Normal Form. There are no repeating groups, and each row can be uniquely identified by a primary key (in this case, a composite key). Therefore, this table adheres to the rules of 1NF. One of the attributes (DatePublished) is not dependent on the whole composite key, but only on a part of it (TitleID); therefore, this violates the rules for 2NF.

QUESTION 5
The correct answer is C. A single statement is already protected against hardware failure, since it is run in an implicit transaction. Error handling and grouping multiple statements are valid reasons for using explicit transactions.

QUESTION 6
The correct answer is D: a table can have multiple unique constraints, but only one primary key. Answer A is incorrect, because these are not synonyms. Answer B is incorrect, because a foreign key can reference both unique constraints and primary keys (as we've shown in the examples). Answer C is incorrect, because the opposite is true: a unique constraint allows a single NULL value, a primary key does not

QUESTION 7
The correct answer is A: REFERENCES. For the exact syntax, see the code samples.

QUESTION 8
The correct answer is C: INTERSECT. When you combine two queries using INTERSECT, this will show the records in both result sets. UNION combines both result sets, eliminating duplicates; UNION ALL will combine both result sets without

eliminating duplicates; and EXCEPT will show the records in the first result set that do not appear in the second result set.

QUESTION 9
The correct answer is A: LEFT OUTER JOIN. Right outer join would have been OK too, but this answer is not listed. An INNER JOIN would not report products without a sale. A UNION of UNION ALL would not produce the correct report.

QUESTION 10
The correct answer is A: not normalized. No combination of attributes can be used to uniquely identify every record. This is one of the first requirements for 1NF (the other one: no repeating groupings).
By the way: the question adds some irrelevant information. The relevant attributes are not Gender and DateOfBirth. Adding irrelevant information to a question is a technique that is often used in exam questions: you have to be able to decide what information is relevant.

Chapter 4: Views, stored procedures and functions

Chapter overview
In this chapter, we introduce some additional programmability features.

Preview
In the preceding chapters, we've installed SQL, designed and created tables and learned how to put data in, and gotten it out again using T-SQL. In this chapter, we're going to learn four new constructs: views, stored procedures, triggers and functions. The primary use of these constructions is not to allow you to do new things (except for user defined functions and triggers), but they do give you a lot more flexibility in the way you can achieve the same result. They are also useful for security.

Key concepts
Views, stored procedures, functions, triggers

Requirements
You need access to a test database with database owner (dbo) privileges.

Exam objectives
For the exam, the relevant objectives are:
* Understand data definition language (DDL). understanding how T-SQL can be used to create database objects such as tables and views.
* Create views.
* Understanding when to use views and how to create a view by using T-SQL or a graphical designer.
* Create stored procedures and functions.

Views

A view is a virtual table, whose contents are defined by a query. The view itself does not store any data; this data is still stored in the underlying table(s). There are two main reasons to use views:
* To allow for easier coding (better readability);
* To provide granular security.

Let's start with an example of a view. In the previous chapter, we've seen the use of a subquery in the FROM clause:

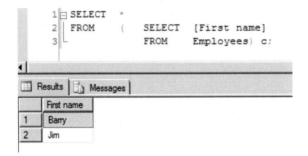

This was obviously a contrived example; there is no point in selecting everything from a subquery without further manipulation. This example was meant to demonstrate the syntax of the subquery, not the usefulness.

Code like this, containing subqueries, can be hard to read when the code gets more complex. To make life easier for the developer, this subquery can be stored as a view. We can create a view that contains only the contents of the subquery:

```
CREATE VIEW vwEmployeeFirstName
AS
SELECT [first name]
FROM    Employees;
```

Now, we can select from the view just as we did from the subquery:

```
SELECT  *
FROM    vwEmployeefirstname;
```

In this simple example, the original code was not so very complex, so substituting the subquery for a view doesn't make that much of a difference. For subqueries that join several tables, it does start to matter. The join example from chapter 3 would be a better query to substitute with a view:

```
CREATE VIEW vwCustomers
AS
SELECT [First name]
      ,[Last name]
      ,Address
      ,OrderDate
      ,[Order line number]
      ,Item
      ,quantity
```

[80]

```
           ,price
FROM   Customers c
       JOIN Orders o ON c.CustomerID = o.CustomerID
       JOIN Orderlines ol on ol.OrderID = o.OrderID;
```

Substituting this query with a view would actually be useful to improve readability. The second reason to use a view is security. You can grant SELECT permissions to a view without granting permissions to the underlying tables. We'll cover security in chapter 6, but for now, it is sufficient to know that you have to grant a user permission to select data from a table, otherwise the user is not allowed to do so.

Building on the previous example, let's say you have a sales representative that is allowed to see customer information, but only from customers from London. Granting SELECT permission on the entire table would enable him to see customers from other areas as well. Granting permission on a view with only the London customers, without granting permission to the table would accomplish this goal. This is the syntax to create this view:

```
CREATE VIEW vwLondonCustomers
AS
SELECT [First name]
           ,[Last name]
           ,Address
           ,OrderDate
           ,[Order line number]
           ,Item
           ,quantity
           ,price
FROM   Customers c
       JOIN Orders o ON c.CustomerID = o.CustomerID
       JOIN Orderlines ol on ol.OrderID = o.OrderID
WHERE   c.Address LIKE '%London%';
```

Or, alternatively, we could build this view on top of the previous view:

```
CREATE VIEW vwLondonCustomers
AS
SELECT *
FROM   vwCustomers
WHERE   Address LIKE '%London%';
```

This saves a lot of typing if you need to make a view for several areas. Be aware that building views on top of views makes troubleshooting more difficult, so many DBA's frown upon this; you're probably building spaghetti code that nobody can unravel.

The next step would be to give read permissions on this newly created view to the sales representative. We'll show you how to do that in chapter 6.

Unfortunately, the attribute "address" we've used in the WHERE clause, is a single field, and not separated into street name, house number and city. Therefore, this view could also contain records of customers living in London Street (there is probably a London Street somewhere out there). In chapter 2 we said that in the real world, storing "address" as a single field wasn't a good idea; here you can see one reason why.

Some sales organizations are really careful about customer information, even within the organization, and with good reason. When an account manager leaves the company, it is quite tempting to take as much customer information as possible to their next job. It is a security best practice to grant access to the necessary information, and nothing more.

We've now seen how to create a view using T-SQL. You can also create views with the graphical designer. The result is the same, but the exam requires that you know both methods. So we'll drop the view first:

```
DROP VIEW vwLondonCustomers
```

Now, we can create the view with the graphical designer:
* Go to Object Explorer;
* Open your test database;
* Right-click on "Views", click "New View…";
* Select both the "Customers" table and the "Orders" table (by holding down the shift key), and click "Add". These are the tables that will provide the data for the view. As you can see, you can also select other views or functions. In the upper part of the screen, you'll see the three tables with the relationships between them.
* Check the box to select the appropriate columns.
* Add the filter for address (LIKE '%London%'). The screen should now look like the screenshot below.
* Close this tab to save the view.

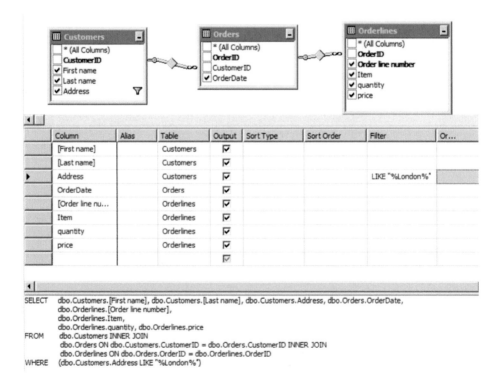

Both methods of creating a view (T-SQL and the graphical designer) will produce the same result. However, using a script is preferable because you can save and reuse the script.

There are several more things you have to know about views:
* You can't use an ORDER BY when creating the view; however, you can, and should, use ORDER BY when querying the view.

[82]

* The name of the columns from the view will be the same name as the column it was derived from, unless you use a column alias (as seen in chapter 2) in T-SQL, or the "alias" column in the graphical designer.
* Each column in the view requires a distinct name. So you will have to use a column alias when joining tables that have a column with the same name, or when a column is computed (an example of this is the concatenation of first name and last name).

This is all you need to know about views for the exam.

Stored procedures

A stored procedure is a small T-SQL program stored inside the database. This can be a single T-SQL statement, or a collection of statements. There are lots of reasons to create a stored procedure:
* To allow for easier coding (especially code reuse);
* To enhance performance. Each time SQL executes a statement, it has to devise a plan how to execute this statement as fast as possible (this is called the execution plan). This plan will be stored in memory. The execution plan of a stored procedure can be reused the next time the stored proc is executed; this may not be the case for code executed outside a stored procedure. Reuse of an execution plan is beneficial, since calculating an execution plan can be quite expensive (in terms of CPU time).
* To provide granular security. As with a view, you can grant a user the permission to execute a stored procedure without granting permissions on the underlying tables. And as with the view, we'll talk more about this in chapter 6.
* To perform complex checks and error handling.

We'll first show you an easy example of a stored procedure, before we introduce the option that really causes stored procedures to shine: parameters.
Here is how to create a stored procedure that selects customer information:

```
CREATE PROC procGetCustomerInformation
AS
BEGIN
        --explanation of what the stored proc does
        SET NOCOUNT ON;
        SELECT *
        FROM    Customers;
END
```

"CREATE PROC" is short for "CREATE PROCEDURE"; both do the same. The "BEGIN" and "END" keywords are optional; so is the "SET NOCOUNT ON". Both, however, are best practices, so we'll include them here. The "SET NOCOUNT ON" prevents SQL from returning the message "x rows affected" to the client; this information is almost always ignored, so "SET NOCOUNT ON" prevents this network overhead (and thereby improves performance just a little bit).
The line of commentary may be optional from a technical perspective, but by many developers it is considered mandatory. Because the stored procedure gets stored in the database, it can be especially helpful to add comments. For example, you might put in things like:
* What the stored proc is supposed to do;
* Special attention to parts of the code that are not straightforward;
* The date the stored proc was written;

* The name of the developer who wrote it;
* The version of the stored proc;
* Changes in this version.

Our example stored procedure can be executed as follows:

```
EXEC procGetCustomerInformation;
```

The result is the same as the SELECT statement inside the stored proc. Notice that the messages tab now does not have the message "(4 row(s) affected)", but instead a simple "Command(s) completed successfully." (due to the command SET NOCOUNT ON).

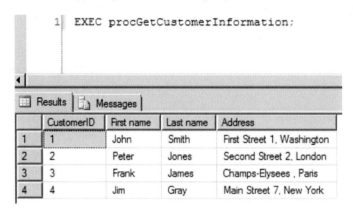

"EXEC" is short for "EXECUTE"; both do the same. The DDL code to delete the stored procedure is very familiar:

```
DROP PROC procGetCustomerInformation;
```

All this is pretty straightforward. Things become really interesting when you start to use parameters. A parameter is a variable that can be used to store a single value. This value can then be manipulated and used to compare with data attributes, variables or other parameters. As with a column, a parameter has to be declared with a data type.
Parameters can be either optional or mandatory, and used for either input into the stored proc, or output from the stored proc.
In the following example, we'll create a stored proc to retrieve the ID of a customer.

```
CREATE PROC procGetCustomerID
        @FirstName varchar(100)
        ,@LastName varchar(100)
        ,@Address     varchar(100)
AS
BEGIN
        SET NOCOUNT ON;
        SELECT CustomerID
        FROM        Customers
        WHERE  [First name] = @FirstName
                    AND [Last name] = @LastName
                    AND [Address] = @Address;
END;
```

[84]

Two things about the parameter declaration. First, note that we've used the same data type for the parameters as the column definition. This decreases the chances of errors; if the column would allow 200 characters, and the corresponding parameter only 100, you could get errors. Second, we've given each parameter a descriptive name. It may be tempting to name your variables @1, @2 and @3, but avoid doing this; otherwise, larger pieces of code will become unreadable.

To execute this stored proc, you have to supply a value for each parameter.

```
1   EXEC procGetCustomerID
```
Procedure or function 'procGetCustomerID' expects parameter '@FirstName', which was not supplied.

While typing, Intellisense will help you with the parameters you need to supply. There are two ways of supplying the values for the parameters, explicit and implicit.

```
EXEC procGetCustomerID
     @firstname = 'Jim'
     ,@lastname = 'Gray'
     ,@address = 'Main Street 7, New York';
```

```
EXEC procGetCustomerID
     'Jim'
     ,'Gray'
     ,'Main Street 7, New York';
```

In the first example, we've explicitly given the parameter names as well as the values; in the second example we've only given the parameter values. If you supply a value for each parameter, in the correct order, it is optional to supply the parameter names (however, for readability it is better to make things explicit). In this case, all parameters are mandatory, so you need to supply a value; otherwise, you'll get an error, for example if you omit the value for address:

Msg 201, Level 16, State 4, Procedure procGetCustomerID, Line 0
Procedure or function 'procGetCustomerID' expects parameter '@Address', which was not supplied.

A parameter can be made optional by declaring it with a default value:

```
CREATE PROC procGetCustomerID
     @FirstName varchar(100) = 'Jim'
     ,@LastName varchar(100) = NULL
     ...
```

The preceding parameters were all input parameters. Now let's look at an output parameter. You can define an output parameter simply by using the keyword "OUTPUT" (or "OUT"). Then, in the body of the stored proc, you have to assign a value to this parameter (if you don't supply a value to this output parameter, it will still work, but it doesn't make any sense to return an empty output parameter).

Let's change our stored proc to add an output parameter. Because the stored procedure already exists, we have to either drop it first, or use "ALTER" instead of "CREATE". The difference between ALTER and DROP & CREATE is that the former maintains all permissions, and the latter does not.

```
ALTER PROC procGetCustomerID
        @FirstName varchar(100)
        ,@LastName varchar(100)
        ,@Address     varchar(100)
        ,@CustomerID int OUTPUT
AS
BEGIN
        SET NOCOUNT ON;
        SELECT @CustomerID = CustomerID
        FROM    Customers
        WHERE   [First name] = @FirstName
                    AND [Last name] = @LastName
                    AND [Address] = @Address;
END;
```

To execute the stored proc, you have to create a variable to capture the output:

```
DECLARE @CustomerID int;

EXEC procGetCustomerID
        @firstname = 'Jim'
        ,@lastname = 'Gray'
        ,@address = 'Main Street 7, New York'
        ,@CustomerID = @CustomerID OUTPUT;

SELECT @CustomerID;
```

It might be confusing that @CustomerID gets declared twice: once in the stored proc, and once in the batch that calls the stored proc. To be more precise: it is not one variable declared twice, but two different variables for the same purpose (and therefore we've given them the same name). This has to do with the *scope* of the variable. The variables that are declared in the stored proc can only be used inside the stored procedure, and in the execute statement. It is said that the variable is local to the stored proc (local scope). We've now seen how to use parameters as input and output. Parameters can also be used to control the flow of logic inside a stored procedure.

```
CREATE PROC procLogicalTest
        @parameter int
AS
BEGIN
        SET NOCOUNT ON;
        IF @parameter = 1
        BEGIN
                EXEC proc1;
        END
        ELSE
        BEGIN
```

```
              EXEC proc2
       END
END;
```

We haven't covered logical flow, and neither does the exam, but this example is included anyway because it begins to show the power of stored procedures in combination with parameters. Probably the example is self-explanatory: stored procedure "procLogicalTest" will call either "proc1" or "proc2", based on the value of "@parameter".

This logical flow can also be used for input validation, and correcting minor errors. Let's say you want to use a stored procedure to insert the name of a new customer. Before inserting the name, you can check whether the name has been entered with any leading or trailing spaces, and remove those automatically (using the functions LTRIM and RTRIM; we haven't covered these yet, but we'll get to them later on).

That's it. We've shown that a stored procedure is simply a collection of T-SQL statements, used with or without parameters. Before we move on to functions, some last remarks about stored procedures:

Do not use the prefix sp_ for stored procedures. This prefix is reserved for SQL Server system stored procedures. In our examples we've used the prefix "proc" as naming convention. Having a consistent naming convention helps to make code more readable. You can't use "GO" in a stored procedure. This is a batch separator, and all statements inside a stored procedure are executed in a single batch. Neither can you use the "USE database" clause to switch database. If you do need to access another database, you should reference the table as [database].[schema].[table] (with or without the square brackets).

Functions

A function is a SQL statement that accepts an input parameter, performs an action using this parameter and returns a value (either a single value or a result set). Based on this description, you might wonder what the difference is between a function and a stored procedure. There are several differences, in usage, capabilities and performance. For now, the most important ones are:

* A function *must* return a value; a stored procedure *may* return a value, or even more than one.
* A function cannot be used to perform actions to change the database state (that is: you can't perform DML such as inserts, updates or deletes to change data).
* Stored procedures can be executed on their own (as we've seen) using "EXECUTE", while functions are executed as part of a SQL statement.

There are two kinds of functions: user-defined functions and system functions (sometimes called built-in functions). We'll start by showing how to use a function, using system functions as an example. Then we'll show you how to create a user-defined function.

In chapter 2 we talked about data types, and said that SQL easily allows you to add one month to a date, provided that you store that date as a datetime data type (not as a string data type). This can be accomplished using a function: the system function "DATEADD".

Suppose you allow customers one month to pay, and you want to calculate when payment is due for an order. So let's add one month to the "OrderDate":

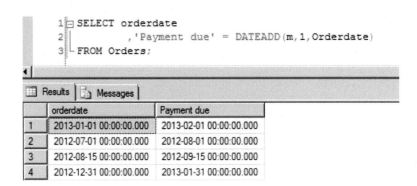

```
1  SELECT orderdate
2         , 'Payment due' = DATEADD(m,1,Orderdate)
3  FROM Orders;
```

	orderdate	Payment due
1	2013-01-01 00:00:00.000	2013-02-01 00:00:00.000
2	2012-07-01 00:00:00.000	2012-08-01 00:00:00.000
3	2012-08-15 00:00:00.000	2012-09-15 00:00:00.000
4	2012-12-31 00:00:00.000	2013-01-31 00:00:00.000

The function "DATEADD" requires three arguments:
* The interval (in this case: m for month);
* The number of intervals to add (in this case: 1);
* The date to which to add something (in this case: "OrderDate").

If you want to know the details of this function, such as the other available interval options, highlight it in SSMS and press F1 to open BooksOnline. Don't look for "DATESUBTRACT", as this doesn't exist; to subtract, use a negative number of intervals.
There are a lot of system functions. In SSMS, you can find the available functions in each database under Programmability, divided into categories (see screenshot). It can be quite useful to browse through these functions, because the built-in functions can be used to solve a lot of SQL problems. It's not at all unusual for developers and database administrators to spend hours on a problem, that could have easily been solved with a built-in function. Even if there is no built-in functions to solve your problem in the current version of SQL, it might be included in the next version if enough developers have the same problem.

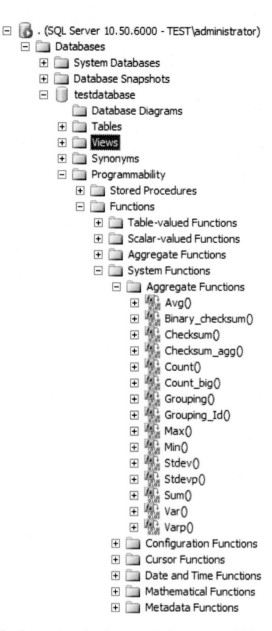

The three categories that contain the most useful functions are:
* Aggregate functions;
* Date and Time functions;
* String functions.

We'll give a short example of each of these system functions. First, the aggregate functions.

```
1 ⊟ SELECT    'Average' = AVG(quantity)
2            ,'Average #2' = AVG(CAST(quantity as decimal(5,2)))
3            ,'Number' = COUNT(*)
4            ,'Maximum' = MAX(quantity)
5 ⊦          ,'Minimum' = MIN(quantity)
6 ⊟          ,'Total' = SUM(quantity)
7 ⌐ FROM     Orderlines;
```

Results | Messages

	Average	Average #2	Number	Maximum	Minimum	Total
1	3	3.500000	4	10	1	14

Note the average, as calculated in line 1. The total number of items ordered is 14; divided by 4 , this should return 3.5, but it doesn't. This is because "quantity" is an integer. The end result of the manipulation of a parameter (or a field) is usually a parameter of the same data type as the original. So, 14 divided by 4 becomes 3 unless we first change the datatype by casting "quantity", in this case to decimal(5,2). We've done just that for "Average #2". The rest of the functions should be self-evident.
Next up are the date & time functions.

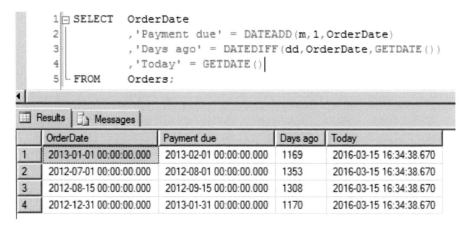

```
1 ⊟ SELECT    OrderDate
2            ,'Payment due' = DATEADD(m,1,OrderDate)
3            ,'Days ago' = DATEDIFF(dd,OrderDate,GETDATE())
4            ,'Today' = GETDATE()|
5 ⌐ FROM     Orders;
```

Results | Messages

	OrderDate	Payment due	Days ago	Today
1	2013-01-01 00:00:00.000	2013-02-01 00:00:00.000	1169	2016-03-15 16:34:38.670
2	2012-07-01 00:00:00.000	2012-08-01 00:00:00.000	1353	2016-03-15 16:34:38.670
3	2012-08-15 00:00:00.000	2012-09-15 00:00:00.000	1308	2016-03-15 16:34:38.670
4	2012-12-31 00:00:00.000	2013-01-31 00:00:00.000	1170	2016-03-15 16:34:38.670

Finally, the string functions.

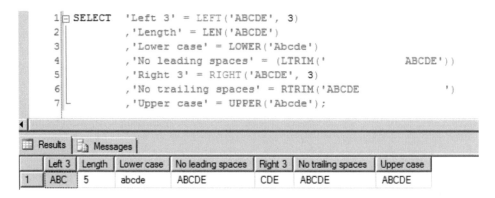

```
1 ⊟ SELECT    'Left 3' = LEFT('ABCDE', 3)
2            ,'Length' = LEN('ABCDE')
3            ,'Lower case' = LOWER('Abcde')
4            ,'No leading spaces' = (LTRIM('          ABCDE'))
5            ,'Right 3' = RIGHT('ABCDE', 3)
6            ,'No trailing spaces' = RTRIM('ABCDE          ')
7 ⌐          ,'Upper case' = UPPER('Abcde');
```

Results | Messages

	Left 3	Length	Lower case	No leading spaces	Right 3	No trailing spaces	Upper case
1	ABC	5	abcde	ABCDE	CDE	ABCDE	ABCDE

These should explain themselves. In the section about stored procs, we talked about the possibility to create a stored proc that would remove leading and trailing spaces to customer information before inserting it in the customer table. Can you now create and test this stored proc? Hint: to remove both leading and trailing spaces, you'll have to nest the LTRIM and RTRIM functions, like this: LTRIM(RTRIM(' Bill ')).

Now we've seen system functions, let's create our own function. There are two types of functions: scalar and table. Scalar functions, like the scalar subquery we saw earlier, return a single value; table functions return a table. We'll create a scalar function that doubles a number. This is really quite easy to do.

```
1  CREATE FUNCTION fnDoubler (@input INT)
2  RETURNS INT
3  AS
4  BEGIN
5      SET @input = @input * 2;
6      RETURN @input
7  END
```

Note that we don't have to give a name to the output, like we had to do for the output parameters of a stored procedure. Because a function must have one, and only one result, it is always clear which result we're interested in, and therefore it would be superfluous to give that result a name. We only have to specify the data type (or "TABLE" if the function returns a result set).

The way to use the function in a select statement is the same as with the system functions, except that we need to specify the schema the function is created in (in this case, dbo). Unlike with a stored procedure, parameters are not called by name.

```
1  SELECT '16 * 2 = ' = dbo.fndoubler(16);
```

	16 * 2 =
1	32

The DDL statements to drop or alter a function are simply DROP and ALTER.

Triggers

A trigger is a special type of stored procedure that is automatically executed after a predefined event occurs in the database. For example, the following trigger would log an entry to an audit table whenever someone updates a sales order:

```
CREATE TRIGGER [dbo].[trOrderUpdate] ON [dbo].[Orders]
AFTER UPDATE
AS
BEGIN
        INSERT Logging (LogTime, LogMessage)
        VALUES (GETDATE(), 'Orders table has been updated');
END;
```

This triggers executes (fires) automatically when anybody updates the sales order table. To be actually useful, we'd have to add some additional logic to this trigger. In the exercise at the end of this section, we'll create two triggers: one to update the logging table with the before and after value of the update, and one to rollback the update if the new value is not to our liking. But first we'll cover a bit more theory about triggers.

Types of triggers
There are three types of triggers: DML, DDL and logon triggers. The difference is the type of event that has to happen in order to fire the trigger. As you might have guessed from the name, a DML trigger fires after a specific DML event, etc.
DDL and logon triggers always fire *after* the event; a DML trigger is to be performed either *after* the event happens, or *instead of* the event, depending on the trigger definition. In the example above, the update is executed and after that, the record gets inserted into the logging table, because the trigger has been defined as "after update". If the trigger had been defined as "instead of update", the update would not have occurred, but the trigger would still have fired to log the attempted update.
A trigger and the action that caused the trigger are performed in a single transaction. Because of this, you can cause the code of the trigger to rollback the action (for example, based on the data that is inserted). We'll see an example of this later on.

The deleted and inserted table
One very useful feature of DML triggers is that triggers have access to both the old and new data. In the case of a delete trigger, the deleted data; in the case of an insert, the inserted data; and in the case of an update trigger, both the inserted and deleted data. This is through tables called "deleted" and "inserted". They only exist within the scope of the trigger, and have the same structure as the table on which the trigger is created. Consider our Customer table. It has a column called "FirstName". The following code sample shows how to access the old value for FirstName within an update trigger:

```
. . .
        SELECT FirstName
        FROM   deleted
. . .
```

A word of caution when firing triggers
There are some potential issues to be aware of when using triggers in SQL Server (though not as potentially lethal as in real life).
The first is that triggers are not meant to be used to return result sets to the user; this is by design. Actually, the ability to return results will probably be removed in a future version of SQL Server. So returning results to the user might work, but don't do it: you should never build solutions on unsupported features.
The second is that an error in a trigger can cause the transaction to be rolled back, and since the trigger is executed in the same transaction as the original event, thereby causing the event to be rolled back as well. For example, an error in a logon trigger can prevent users from logging on.
A third issue is of a more practical nature. Triggers tend to be overlooked when troubleshooting, since a trigger is the unintentional side effect of an intended action. When creating triggers, it is especially important to thoroughly test its effects, and if you have more than one trigger, you have to be mindful of the interaction of these triggers. The execution of a trigger on one object can cause the firing of a trigger on another object, and if you have more than one trigger on the same object, the order of execution

[92]

of these triggers might become important. For more on the interaction of triggers, see the link in the section "Further reading".

All this doesn't mean you should not use triggers; a trigger is just a tool, and like every other tool, should be used appropriately. We'll show you how to use this tool in the following exercises.

Exercises

You have an order table with an order date. Create a trigger for every update on this order table. The trigger should record the old order date, the new order date and the time of the update in a logging table.

```
CREATE TABLE [dbo].[Orders](
        [OrderID] [int] NOT NULL,
        [Customer] [varchar](100) NULL,
        [Orderdate] [smalldatetime] NOT NULL,
PRIMARY KEY CLUSTERED
([OrderID] ASC));
```

Update a record in the order table. Notice the Messages tab. How can you tell the trigger was executed?

Add a check to the trigger: if the new order date is in the future, do not allow the update. Now drop the logging table, and perform another update on the sales table. What happens?

Exercise solution
First, let's create the logging table.

```sql
CREATE TABLE [dbo].[Logging] (
        LogTime                 smalldatetime
        , LogMessage  varchar(1000)
        , OldValue              smalldatetime
        , NewValue              smalldatetime);
```

A few comments about this table. First: there is no need to normalize this table. You could add an identity column, though, to make each record uniquely identifiable. Second: since [Orders].[Orderdate] is a smalldatetime, so should the columns for OldValue and NewValue.

Another possible solution would be to incorporate the old and new value into the log message.

Next, we're going to have to create a trigger. For LogTime, we'll use system function "getdate()" (as we've seen in the section about functions). For OldValue and NewValue, we need to access the tables "inserted" and "deleted".

```sql
CREATE TRIGGER [dbo].[trOrderUpdate] ON [dbo].[Orders]
AFTER UPDATE
AS
BEGIN
        INSERT Logging (LogTime, LogMessage, OldValue, NewValue)
        SELECT          GETDATE()
                        , 'Orders table has been updated'
                        , deleted.orderdate
                        , inserted.Orderdate
        FROM deleted, inserted
END;
```

In the Object Explorer, this is where you can find the trigger:

- Tables
  - System Tables
  - dbo.AuthorTitle
  - dbo.Customers
  - dbo.Employees
  - dbo.Orderlines
  - dbo.Orders
    - Columns
    - Keys
    - Constraints
    - Triggers
      - trOrderUpdate
    - Indexes
    - Statistics
  - dbo.Persons
  - dbo.Shipments

To make the resulting message even more useful, we could have included the name of the user who made the update, using another system function:

```
. . .
        , 'Orders table has been updated by ' + SUSER_NAME()
. . .
```

But that wasn't a requirement. Now, let's test the trigger:

```
INSERT ORDERS
VALUES (1, 'Bob', GETDATE());

UPDATE ORDERS
SET Orderdate = GETDATE ()
WHERE orderid = 1;

SELECT * FROM logging;
```

The message tab shows the effect of the trigger. Even though only one record is updated in the [orders] table, the trigger causes another record to be affected in the [LogMessage] table:

```
(1 row(s) affected)

(1 row(s) affected)
```

Next, we'll check to see if the date isn't in the future. To do this, we'll use an "if-then-else" construction. We'll check the value for [inserted].[orderdate] against system time.

```
ALTER TRIGGER [dbo].[trOrderUpdate] ON [dbo].[Orders]
AFTER UPDATE
AS
BEGIN
        IF EXISTS (    SELECT orderdate
                       FROM   inserted
                       WHERE  orderdate > GETDATE())
        BEGIN
                ROLLBACK
        END
        ELSE
        BEGIN
                INSERT Logging (LogTime, LogMessage, OldValue,
                NewValue)
                SELECT GETDATE()
                       , 'Orders table has been updated'
                       , deleted.orderdate
                       , inserted.Orderdate
                FROM   deleted, inserted;
        END
END;
```

[95]

To test the triggers functionality, let's try to change the order date to tomorrow's date:

```
UPDATE Orders
SET    OrderDate = DATEADD(dd, 1, GETDATE())
WHERE  OrderId = 1
```

The trigger caused the entire transaction to be rolled back. Now, let's drop the logging table, and rerun the update statement (with an order date in the past). The statement fails, because the trigger tries to update the table we've just deleted:

```
Msg 208, Level 16, State 1, Procedure trOrderUpdate, Line 26
Invalid object name 'Logging'.
```

This exercise demonstrated the use and the risks of using triggers.

Summary

In this chapter, we've seen the view, the stored procedure, the function and the trigger. A view is a virtual table, whose contents are defined by a query. A stored procedure is a small T-SQL program stored inside the database; you can use stored procedures with or without parameters, either input or output. A function is also a small T-SQL program stored inside the database, but unlike a stored procedure, it cannot alter the database, and must return exactly one table or value. A trigger is a special type of stored procedure that is automatically executed after a predefined DML, DDL or logon event.

Further reading

You can define multiple triggers on a table. To understand how they would interact, read the following MSDN article:

https://msdn.microsoft.com/en-us/library/ms189799.aspx

Questions

QUESTION 1
To prevent orders from being deleted, you want to implement a trigger. Which type of trigger do you need?

A Before update DML trigger
B Instead of update DML trigger
C After update DML trigger
D After update DDL trigger
E This can't be done with a trigger. Use a stored procedure instead.

QUESTION 2
Which of the following provides the ability to perform several actions as one, protecting against system failure?

A Database security
B Stored procedures
C Transactions
D Views

QUESTION 3
You have a table with exam results. Possible values for results range from 0 to 100. You want to limit the range of possible values for the attribute. What is the best way to achieve this?

A Stored proc
B Foreign key
C View
D Check constraint

QUESTION 4
Which keyword should be added on line 1?

```
1  CREATE ... dbo.AmountVAT (@Price dec(18,2))
2  RETURNS dec(18,2)
3  AS
4  BEGIN
5      SET @Price = @Price * 0.06
6      RETURN @Price
7  END;
```

A Proc
B Trigger
C View
D Functions

QUESTION 5
You are the database administrator for a large company. Recently, a developer added a table in production without informing you. In the future, you want to notified when this happens. How can you achieve this?

A Stored proc
B System function
C Trigger
D Logon auditing

QUESTION 6
Which line of code contains a syntax error?

```
1  CREATE VIEW [dbo].[vwHappyAnniversary]
2  AS
3  SELECT  *
4  FROM    Persons
5  WHERE   DATEPART(day,DateOfBirth) = DATEPART(day,GETDATE())
6          and DATEPART(month, DateOfBirth) = DATEPART(month,GETDATE())
7  ORDER BY DateOfBrith DESC
```

A Line 1
B Line 3
C Line 5
D Line 7

QUESTION 7
Which is not a good reason to use stored procedures?

A Code reuse
B Improved database performance
C More granular security
D Faster application development

Answers

QUESTION 1
The correct answer is B. An update statement is DML, and the trigger has to be an "instead of" trigger. There is no such thing as a before trigger. It is possible to use an after update DML trigger (answer C) with a rollback, but answer C does not form a complete solution and is therefore incorrect.

QUESTION 2
The correct answer is C. Transactions serve to treat several actions as a single unit of work. Database security protects against unauthorized actions, but not against system failure. Stored procedures can be used with transactions, but not necessarily; views and stored procedures do not protect against system failure.

QUESTION 3
The correct answer is D. A check constraint is the best way to limit the range of possible values.
A stored procedure can limit the possible range of values that can be inserted for an attribute, but unless data entry into the table can only be performed through this stored procedure, this does not accomplish the required result. A foreign key to an attribute in a another table with values 0-100 would accomplish the required result, but it is not the best way, as this requires more work than necessary. A view cannot be used to limit the range of possible data values in a table.

QUESTION 4
The correct answer is D: function. A stored procedure uses input and output parameters to return data, not RETURNS. A trigger would require the description of the action that fires the trigger, and should not return data. A view does not use input.

QUESTION 5
The correct answer is C: a trigger. A DDL trigger could accomplish this. Neither a stored procedure or a system function would be executed on the event of a table creation. Logon auditing, though we haven't covered this yet, only audits logon events (as the name implies).

QUESTION 6
The correct answer is D: a view can't be made with an ORDER BY clause. The other lines are correct.

QUESTION 7
The correct answer is D: faster application development. Modern development frameworks have the capability of generating SQL code for the developer; replacing this generated code with stored procedures takes extra effort on the part of the developer. The other answers are good reasons for using stored procedures (see the introduction of the section on stored procs).

Chapter 5: Indexes

Chapter overview
In this chapter, we're going to deal with one of the most important aspects of database performance: the index.

Preview
In previous chapters, we've already seen some aspects that impact the performance of the database, such as selecting an appropriate level of normalization, choosing the smallest possible data type and selecting only the data you actually need. In this chapter, we're going to deal with one of the most important aspects of database performance: the index. Especially with large databases, it is important to add the right indexes. First, we'll give you a conceptual understanding of indexes; then, we'll show them in action. To do that, we'll add an index and compare query performance with and without the index. Some parts of indexing will be explained more than once, but indexing is a difficult yet very important topic; therefore we will explain some parts from several angles. For the same reason, we will go a bit deeper than needed for the exam. Even so: the explanations of data structures given in this chapter will be simplifications of the actual structures, as the exact inner workings are beyond the scope of the exam.

Key concepts
clustered index, nonclustered index, heap, key lookup, pages

Requirements
AdventureWorks database

Exam objectives
For the exam, the relevant objectives are:
* Understand indexes: understanding clustered and nonclustered indexes and their purpose in a database

Practice questions
What is an index?
When does an index help performance?
When does an index not help, or even hinder, performance?
What types of indexes are available?

Clustered index

Introduction to indexes

Performance tuning is as much an art as it is a science. Usually, the database administrator is informed of a performance problem when users start complaining that their application has become slow. The problem might be caused by the application, the application server, the network, the database design, SQL Server itself or the database server hardware. Often, a lot of these components can be changed to increase performance. But none of these changes have the potential impact of well-placed index. Changes in hardware can be quite expensive, and changes to the application code often require long testing and implementation procedures; an index can be added in minutes and the right index can, without any cost except disk space, reduce execution times by over 99%.

An index in a database is like an index in a book. If you want to locate all pages that deal with "primary key" in a book, you can either read the entire book cover to cover, or look up "primary key" in the index and find the relevant pages almost instantly. The downside of having an index is that, every time a page in the book is changed, the index has to be updated as well. Therefore, adding an index is a balancing act, and has to be done carefully: having lots of unused indexes can be almost as big a problem as having no indexes at all.

Before we go on, a word of caution: the illustrations of heaps and clustered indexes are simplifications of the actual structures. More detail can be found in the Microsoft documentation.

Heap & clustered index

To understand database indexes, you have to understand five concepts: the heap, the clustered index, the page, the inverted B-tree and the nonclustered index.

A table is either a heap or a clustered index. In a heap, there is no logical ordering of the records. Figure 1 is our customer table as a heap (without the address information; the example doesn't use this field). Every new record will be appended to the end of the list, regardless of the data in the record.

First name: John Last name: Smith	First name: Peter Last name: Jones	First name: Frank Last name: James	First name: Jim Last name: Gray

The alternative to a heap is a clustered index. The difference between a heap and a clustered index is that the records in the clustered index are ordered, according to the clustering key (usually but not necessarily the primary key). By the way: this is a logical order, not necessarily the physical order on disk. Figure 2 is the same customer table with a slight modification: to make it more similar to the heap in Figure 1, we've recreated the table with the clustered index on FirstName. Now, the records are ordered on FirstName, from A-Z.

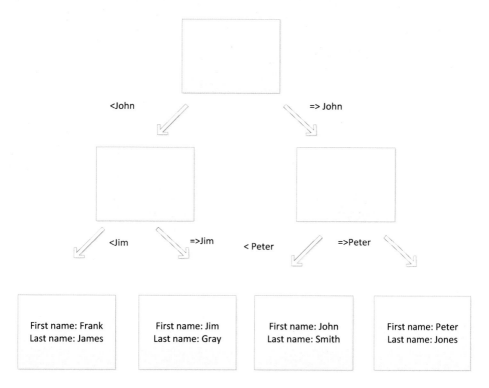

First name: Frank
Last name: James

First name: Jim
Last name: Gray

First name: John
Last name: Smith

First name: Peter
Last name: Jones

Before we'll show the T-SQL code to create this table, just think back to chapter 2, and answer the following question: would it be a good idea to create a clustered index on first name in real life?

```
CREATE TABLE Customers (
        CustomerID int IDENTITY
        ,[First name] varchar(100)
        ,[Last name] varchar(100)
        ,[Address] varchar(100)
        ,PRIMARY KEY ([First name]));
```

Answer: no, it would not, because a primary key value has to be unique, i.e. you can't have two customers with the same first name. Not good for business, but very good for this example, so we'll stick with this primary key.

By default, SQL creates a clustered index on the primary key when you create the table, unless you specify otherwise. Our advice is to choose the clustered index carefully, and only choose a heap if extensive testing shows that it is better in that specific case.

This is another example where the terminology used can be confusing. A clustered index is sometimes called "a table with a clustered index". Other terms you may encounter are base table or HOBT (pronounced hobbit) when referring a table (in cases where it is irrelevant whether it is a heap or a clustered index).

Note that the records are ordered from left to right according to the clustering key, First Name. This is a simplified representation of a clustered index; we'll add more detail to this picture later on. But to do this, we'll have to explain two additional concepts: the B-tree and pages. We'll start with the page.

In SQL Server, records are not stored on disk individually, but on 8 kB chunks called pages. Multiple records can be stored on the same page (if the records are small enough), but a record has to fit entirely on a single page (some of the newer data types can be stored in a separate location, but we won't cover that).

Let's use our customer table as an example, and calculate how many records would fit on a page.

Each record has an int (4 bytes) and 3 varchar(100) columns. There is also some overhead: 2 bytes for each varchar column. So each record is between 10 and 310 bytes. So how big a record actually is depends on the data stored; long names and addresses will take up more space than shorter ones. Let's assume that in our case, the average record is 200 bytes.

An 8kB page is 8096 bytes, but it has 36 bytes of overhead for the page header, so there are 8060 bytes available for data records. Assuming an average size of 200 bytes, 8060 / 200 = 40.3 records fit on a single page, but since an entire record has to fit on the same page, this becomes 40.

The four records in our example table would all fit on a single page. With only a single page, there is not a lot of practical difference between a heap and a clustered index, since all entries would fit onto this one page. So, to be able to illustrate the usefulness of indexes, we'll have a lot more records in our customer table, at least enough to fill 2 pages.

By the way: the performance gain of indexes is negligible in small databases, but gets bigger as the database grows. A lack of useful indexes will not be apparent in a small database. This is one reason a database may get slower over time. Having a good indexing strategy is one way to resolve this problem; cleaning up or archiving old data may be another solution; doing both may be best.

The moment we add enough records to require a second page, SQL will not only add another page for data, but (only in the case of a clustered index) another page as well.

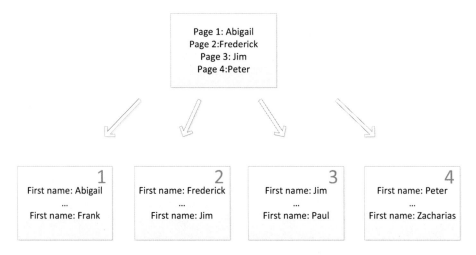

This creates a structure which is called an inverted B-tree (the B stands for Balanced). The levels of the B-tree are named according to the inverted tree analogy: the top level of the B-tree is called the root level; the bottom level, with the actual data, is called the leaf level. If you add enough records, there will come a point where there will be too many pointers to fit on a single page. At that point, an intermediate level will be added, so there will never be more than a single root level page. The root level and the intermediate levels contain pointers to the levels below.

Now we have a root level, SQL will have a different possibility to retrieve data. Let's take two queries and see how SQL would search for a record:

```
SELECT *
FROM    Customers
WHERE   [First name] = 'Jim';

SELECT *
FROM    Customers
WHERE   [Last name] = 'Gray';
```

Both queries search for the same record(s), but in a different way. The first is a search for a record based on the clustered index key; the second is based on an attribute that has no index on it (in our example). SQL would search top-down to find a record based on the clustered index key, in this case first name, starting at the root level. This is called a clustered index seek. To find a record based on last name (or any other attribute), SQL would have to search all records horizontally; this is called a scan (either a clustered index scan or, in the case of a heap, a table scan). According to our simplified version of a clustered index, in a top-down search to find any first name, SQL would need 2 steps; in a horizontal search, SQL would also have to read 2 records. Only when we add enough records to require additional leaf level pages (say another two leaf level pages), the two access patterns will lead to a different amount of work.

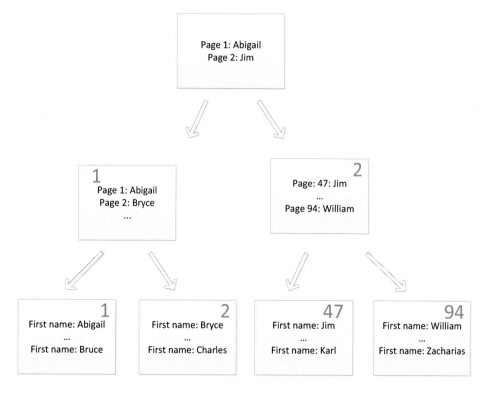

Now, the difference between searching left-to-right or top-down becomes substantial. The top-down search takes 2 steps; the left-to-right search 4 steps. This top-down search is called an *index seek*; the left-to-right search is called a *scan*.

The difference in performance between an index seek and a scan becomes bigger as you add more data pages. With, for example, ten data pages, the seek still requires two pages to be read, while a scan would require ten. Just to reiterate: an index seek can only happen when the index is on a column that is being referenced as a search predicate (in this case: *where [first name] = 'Jim'*).

As we said in chapter 2, choosing the smallest data type matters for performance. This also applies to indexing. The smaller your clustered index field is, the more records you can add to the table before you need another intermediate index level. We now have a clustered index on a varchar(100), which is between 2 and 102 bytes, plus a pointer to the page; therefore, you can fit at least 80 pointers in the root page; this would have been a lot more if we'd have used the CustomerID field (which is a 4 byte integer). In that case, with 94 leaf levels, we'd not need an intermediate level; therefore, a clustered index seek would require one less step.

This inverted B-tree is very scalable. Let's say a root page can reference 400 leaf pages (assuming an average size of 20 bytes for the clustered index field). That means that, with one intermediate level, a root page can reference 400 pages in intermediate level 1, which reference 400 pages on the leaf level; that's 160,000 data pages. Using the clustered index, SQL can locate any record reading just 3 pages (top-down, index seek); without the index, SQL needs to read all 160,000 leaf level pages (left-to-right, scan). Having a clustered index does have a downside to it: the logical ordering has to be maintained. If you insert a record somewhere in the middle, this can lead to a lot of reordering. Nevertheless, a table with a clustered index is faster than a heap in almost every situation.

We've now explained the heap and the clustered index. Looking for data is faster on a clustered index than on a heap, but only if you search for the column on which the clustered index is defined. Now what if you'd like to improve the performance of searches on other columns? For that, we'll move on to the nonclustered index.

Nonclustered index

Unlike the index in the book analogy, the clustered index does not contain a pointer to the data, but instead contains the actual data; the clustered index *is* the table. A nonclustered index is more like the index in a book: it points to the actual data. If the table is a heap, the nonclustered index points to this page directly; if the table is a clustered index, the nonclustered index points to the clustered index field (so SQL will need to go through the B-tree to find the right page, but as we have seen, this will only take a few steps). This does not mean that a nonclustered index performs better on a heap than on a clustered index, but we won't go into this level of detail (we'll see one example later on, though).

There are several differences between a clustered index and a nonclustered index:
* As the clustered index is the actual table, you can only have one clustered index, whereas you can create 999 nonclustered indexes on a table;
* A clustered index is created automatically when you create a table with a primary key, whereas a nonclustered index has to be added explicitly;
* As the clustered index is the actual table, the clustered index is created when you create the table, whereas a nonclustered index can be added or removed at a later time;
* The leaf level of the clustered index contains all of the data, whereas the leaf level of the nonclustered index contains only the indexed column(s) and a pointer to the table (heap or clustered index).

You can create a nonclustered index on one or more columns. We'll give an example of a nonclustered index with a single column:

```
CREATE NONCLUSTERED INDEX [IX_last_name]
ON [dbo].[Customers] ([Last name]);
```

The keyword "NONCLUSTERED" is optional, as nonclustered is the default for creating indexes.

Index usage

Now, when does SQL use this nonclustered index? This depends on a lot of things. The easy answer is that SQL uses this nonclustered index whenever you search for records with a search filter on the column that the index is created on (in this case: last name). Consider the following three queries:

```
SELECT *
FROM    Customers
WHERE   [First name] = 'Jim';

SELECT *
FROM    Customers
WHERE   [Address] LIKE '%Paris%';

SELECT *
FROM    Customers
WHERE   [Last name] = 'Gray';
```

SQL will only use the nonclustered index we've just created ([IX_last_name]) for the third query. SQL will use this nonclustered index to look up the clustered index field of all records that meet the criterion "WHERE [Last name] = 'Gray'", and then look up the remainder of the columns in the table. This last step, where SQL has found the relevant records in the nonclustered index, and needs to look up the remainder of the columns in the base table, is called a key lookup. This key lookup is not necessary if your query only needs information from the columns included in the nonclustered index. For example:

```
SELECT COUNT(*)
FROM    Customers
WHERE   [Last name] = 'Gray';

SELECT [Last name], [First name]
FROM    Customers
WHERE   [Last name] = 'Gray';
```

The first example is easiest: you are not asking for the contents of the records, only the number of records. SQL can answer this question just by looking at the nonclustered index on "last name". The second example requires some explanation. We've created the nonclustered index on last name, and the clustered index is on "First name". Therefore, "First name" is included in the nonclustered index as well ("First Name" is the pointer from the nonclustered index to the table). So if you only request first name and last name, SQL does not need to look up additional attributes in the clustered index.

When we first created this table in chapter 2, we placed the index on "CustomerID"; in that case, SQL would have to perform the key lookup to find "First Name" (using "CustomerID" as the pointer to the table). Had the table been a heap instead of a clustered index, query #2 would require a lookup regardless of which column the primary key was on (this is the example we promised, where a nonclustered index performs better on a clustered index than on a heap).

As an aside: if the table is a heap, the lookup is called a RID lookup, because a heap has an internal structure based on Row Identifiers, or RID. In this text, we won't make this distinction because this is beyond the scope of the exam. In SQL 2000, the generic term for both a key lookup and a RID lookup was a bookmark lookup.

As with the clustered index, the nonclustered index has to be updated whenever one of the columns in the index is updated. This is always the case for an INSERT or DELETE, and for an UPDATE, only when the columns in the index are updated (not when one of the other columns in the table is updated).

This is the performance penalty of having indexes. It is not uncommon to find a table with 5 or 10 nonclustered indexes, and a single INSERT statement will cause an update to all of these indexes. This is where performance tuning can become a balancing act: adding an index to improve one query will slow down other queries. You may have to take into account the relative change in performance, the frequency and the importance of all your queries before you can decide whether or not to implement an additional index. A good starting point is to add indexes on at least all columns that are used to join to other tables (see chapter 3); adding a nonclustered index on every column is usually not a good strategy.

Other aspects of nonclustered indexes that have to be considered are the fact that they take up disk space, and are included in regular maintenance such as backups.

This was the simple answer to the question "When does SQL use this nonclustered index?". The complete answer is that it depends on a lot of things whether SQL decides to use an index or not: the size of the index, other available indexes, and a lot of things we won't cover, such as query hints, parameter sniffing, distribution statistics and connection parameters. Fortunately, though you may not always be able to understand *why* SQL chooses to use an index or not, you can check *whether* SQL chooses to use the index. We'll cover that next.

Indexes in action

To see the effect of an index, we will need a couple of things. First, we'll need a fairly large table. We'll use the "Person" table in the Adventureworks database for this (this table is located in the "Person" schema, so we'll reference it as [Person].[Person]). Second, we'll need to explain two additional concepts: Graphical execution plan and IO statistics.

The query we are going to tune is the following:

```
SELECT *
FROM    Person.Person
WHERE   title = 'Ms';
```

There are different versions of the Adventureworks database available. Maybe your version does not contain the same data as the one we've used. In our version, there is exactly 1 record for a person with title "Ms". To check if the same applies to your version, run the following query:

```
SELECT        title, COUNT(*)
FROM          Person.Person
GROUP BY      title;
```

If your version does not match, just insert a record with a different title and use this in the "WHERE" clause (it is important that only a small percentage of records match the "WHERE" clause, otherwise SQL will not use the index).

Now let's explain the two additional concepts. These are not concepts you'll need to know for the exam, but they will show the effect of the index. Using query execution time is no option, as this depends on a lot of factors (cache, server speed, other processes running at the same time etc.).

In chapter 4, when talking about stored procedures, we already mentioned the execution plan. This is the plan SQL uses internally to execute this statement as fast as possible. One of the decisions SQL has to make when compiling an execution plan, is whether to access the table or an appropriate index. If there are no appropriate nonclustered indexes, SQL has no choice how to execute the query; it has to perform a scan. If there are several indexes available, SQL can choose the best way, either performing a scan or using one (or several) of the available indexes. The resulting execution plan can be made visible; this is called a graphical execution plan. You can do this by selecting the button "Include Actual Execution Plan" in the tool bar before executing a statement.

When we do this for the query we're going to tune, this is the result:

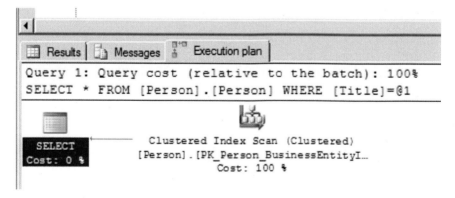

On the result pane, a third tab will show the graphical execution plan. Reading right to left, this execution plan shows that SQL has performed a clustered index scan (not a table scan, as this is not a heap).

Now, let's create the index (this may take some time, depending on the speed of your computer):

```
CREATE INDEX ix_title
ON [person].[person] (title);
```

[109]

And run the query again:

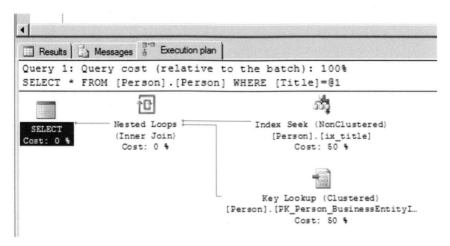

This shows the index in action. SQL has used the index to find the record (in this case only one) that matches the filter. This is the Index Seek. You can see the name of the index, and the table. Then, SQL uses a key lookup to lookup the other columns that belong to that record. Without the key lookup, SQL would only know the values for the clustered index key (and of course the title). If we only wanted these fields, there would be no key lookup necessary. This can be demonstrated with the following query (note that the clustered index is on a column called BusinessEntityID):

```
SELECT title, BusinessEntityID
FROM   Person.Person
WHERE  title = 'Ms';
```

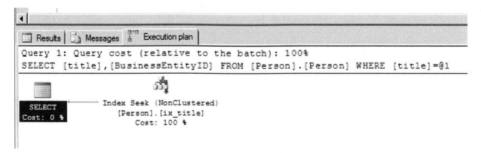

We have now demonstrated that SQL will use the new index to answer this query; we've not shown that this actually helps performance. In our test environment, the query executed in zero seconds with or without the index, so execution time is no indication here. We'll have to look a bit deeper. Often, the main component of query execution time is IO. You can see exactly how much IO is needed for a query by issuing the statement "SET STATISTICS IO ON". First, let's drop the index:

```
DROP INDEX ix_title ON person.person;
```

Now, execute the query again, this time keeping track of IO statistics:

```
SET STATISTICS IO ON;
SELECT *
FROM        Person.Person
WHERE  title = 'Ms';
```

The messages tab will show the IO statistics. You can see 3,816 logical reads in the person table (you can ignore all other stats).

```
◄|
⊞ Results  🗐 Messages  ⌗ Execution plan

(1 row(s) affected)
Table 'Person'. Scan count 1, logical reads 3816, physical reads 0,

(1 row(s) affected)
```

Now, recreate the index and run the query again (including "SET STATISTICS IO ON" is not necessary, this setting is already on for this session):

```
◄|
⊞ Results  🗐 Messages  ⌗ Execution plan

(1 row(s) affected)
Table 'Person'. Scan count 1, logical reads 5, physical reads 0,

(1 row(s) affected)
```

The logical read count is now only 5, down from 3,816. That proves the index helps speed up this query considerably.

By the way: you can use this same method to demonstrate that an insert into a table with a nonclustered index is more work than an insert into the same table but without the nonclustered index. We'll leave this as an exercise to the reader.

Special indexes types

There are three special types of nonclustered indexes we'd like to mention: the filtered index, spatial and XML index.

A filtered index is a nonclustered index that only covers part of the table. This type of index is created by adding a WHERE clause to the create statement:

```
CREATE NONCLUSTERED INDEX [IX_orderdate]
ON [dbo].[Orders] ([Orderdate])
WHERE Orderdate > '2015-01-01'
```

The resulting index will be smaller than a nonfiltered index. A smaller index takes up less space, and is more likely to be used by SQL Server. A filtered index can be useful in situations where most queries are done on a small and clearly defined subset of the data. For example: if an order table has an attribute 'payment received', this attribute will probably be 'true' for the majority of the orders, but the financial department will query unpaid orders more often than paid orders. In that case, an index with a filter on unpaid orders might make sense.

Spatial and XML indexes are indexes on a specific data type: spatial data and XML data, respectively. We didn't cover these data types in chapter two, since they are special purpose data types. Here, we'll shortly mention that the spatial data type is intended for spatial data (usually geographical locations), and XML is loosely structured data. This is what the contents of our Persons table might look like as XML:

```
<persons Firstname="Peter" Lastname="Jones" Address="Second Street
2, London" />
<persons Firstname="Frank" Lastname="James" Address="Champs-Elysees
, Paris" />
<persons Firstname="Jim" Lastname="Gray" Address="Main Street 7, New
York" />
<persons Firstname="John" Lastname="Smith" Address="First Street 1,
Washington" />
```

We won't go into the details of these data types, nor the nature of indexes on these data types. We're just mentioning these indexes so you know there is still a lot more to learn about indexing beyond the types you need to know for the exam: the clustered index, the heap and the nonclustered index.

Summary

At the start of this chapter, we remarked that, in order to give a thorough explanation, we'd go into a lot more detail than needed for the exam. What exactly do you need to know for the exam?

Indexes are used to increase performance. An index seek can be a lot faster than a table scan. These performance gains increase as the size of the database increases. This comes at a cost: indexes increase the size of both the database and the backup, and have to be maintained when modifying data.

A table is either a heap or a clustered index. In a heap, there is no logical ordering of the records; in a clustered index, there is: the records are ordered according to the clustered index key. Because the records are ordered according to the clustered index key, there can only be one clustered index per table. The clustered index key is not necessarily the same as the primary key, but if you create a table with a primary key, SQL will automatically create a clustered index on this primary key (unless you specify a clustered index key). A clustered index is preferable to a heap in almost every situation. A nonclustered index can be created on one or more columns. It does not contain the data for all columns, but only the column it is created on, plus the clustered index key (or a RID pointer, in case of a heap); using this clustered index key (or pointer), SQL can retrieve the corresponding record in the table. You can have as many as 999 nonclustered indexes per table. A nonclustered index will only be used if SQL can use this index to strongly reduce the number of records it needs to read from the table, for example when you reference this table in the WHERE clause, or use it in a join. Other indexes will not be used, but they will still cause overhead, as they have to be maintained for every update, insert and delete.

Further reading

Index internals. As stated, the description given in this chapter is simplified, omitting a lot of details. You can find these details here: (http://msdn.microsoft.com/en-us/library/ms180978(v=sql.105).aspx)

Questions

QUESTION 1
Users note that searching for customer by zip code is slow, while searching by first name or last name is much faster. Which index would be most beneficial to help speed up the search by zip code?

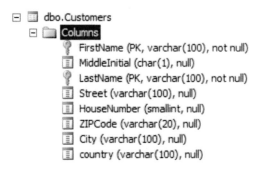

A A clustered index on zip code
B A nonclustered index on zip code and house number
C A nonclustered index on zip code
D A nonclustered index on house number

QUESTION 2
What levels are part of a clustered index?

A Leaf level
B Intermediate level
C RID level
D A and B
E B and C
F None of the above

QUESTION 3
In a nonclustered index on a heap table, what is stored in the leaf level of the index?

A The clustered index key
B It is impossible to create a nonclustered index on an heap table
C The primary key
D The data for all the columns in the table
E The data for the column the nonclustered index was created on

QUESTION 4
You have a log table with the following columns: MessageText, MessageCode, MessageTime. This table is a heap. Thousands of records are added on a daily basis. Every night, data older than 3 years is removed in a batch using the following query:

```
DELETE
FROM [dbo].[Message]
WHERE [messagetime] < DATEADD(y, -3,GETDATE());
```

This nightly batch starts taking longer. You want to speed up this batch by adding an index. Which of the following is the best index to achieve this?

A CREATE INDEX IX_test ON [dbo].[Message] (message);
B CREATE NONCLUSTERED INDEX IX_test ON [dbo].[Message] (message);
C CREATE NONCLUSTERED INDEX IX_test ON [dbo].[Message] (messagetime);
D None of the above. Adding an index will only slow down a delete statement.

QUESTION 5
You have a log table with the following columns: MessageText, MessageCode, MessageTime. This table is a heap. Thousands of records are added on a daily basis. These inserts are taking longer and longer. You want to speed up these inserts by adding an index. Which of the following is the best index to achieve this?

A CREATE INDEX IX_test ON [dbo].[Message] (message);
B CREATE NONCLUSTERED INDEX IX_test ON [dbo].[Message] (message);
C CREATE NONCLUSTERED INDEX IX_test ON [dbo].[Message] (messagetime);
D None of the above. Adding an index will only slow down an insert statement.

QUESTION 6
Which type of index contains the actual data?

A Nonclustered index
B Heap
C Clustered index
D Filtered index

QUESTION 7
A clustered index must be created on an attribute that is unique (for example, the primary key). True or false?

A True
B False

Answers

This section contains the correct answers to the questions, plus an explanation of the wrong answers. In addition to the correct answers, we'll also give a few pointers which are useful on the actual exam.

QUESTION 1
The correct answer is C: a nonclustered index on zip code.
A and B would speed up the search by zip code, but they are not the best answers. A clustered index on zip code would mean dropping the existing clustered index; this would speed up the search on zip code, but slow down the search by name. B contains the additional column, and would therefore be better for a search on zip code & house number, but that is not a requirement in this question. Answer D is wrong, as it doesn't include zip code.

QUESTION 2
Correct answer: D. The leaf level is always included; an intermediate level can be part of an index, given enough records. The term "RID level" is not a correct term. Hint: if you encounter a term you don't recognize, provided that you're properly prepared, it is probably not the correct answer.

QUESTION 3
Correct answer: E. Answer A would be part of the correct answer for a nonclustered index on a clustered index table, not on a heap. The same goes for C (unless the primary key is not the clustered index key). B is wrong, as you can create nonclustered indexes on both heaps and clustered indexes. D is always wrong, unless there is only one column in the table.

QUESTION 4
Correct answer: C. Answers A and B are the same, as the default for the "CREATE INDEX" statement is nonclustered. Adding an index on the column message will not help. D is not correct; even though the index slow down inserts, and will be overhead when actually removing the records, SQL will first need to find which records to remove, which far outweighs the overhead.

QUESTION 5
Correct answer: D. Indexes only hurt INSERT performance.

QUESTION 6
Correct answer: C. A is not correct, as a nonclustered index only contains data for the index keys and the clustered index keys. B is not correct, as a heap is not an index. D is not correct, because a filtered index is a type of nonclustered index.

QUESTION 7
False. A clustered index can be created on an attribute that is not unique.

Chapter 6: Administering a database

Chapter overview
In this final chapter, we'll cover security and database backups.

Preview
While the previous chapters were more relevant to database developers, security and backups are more relevant to database administrators.

In the section on security, we'll talk about SQL authentication and Windows authentication, the difference between users and logons, and how to grant permissions to users, either directly or indirectly (through the use of roles).

In the section of backups, we'll talk about three different types of backup: full, differential and transaction log backup. More importantly, we'll cover restoring these backups. After this, you'll be ready for the exam!

Key concepts
Authentication, authorization, full backup, differential backup, transaction log backup, restore, RPO, RTO

Exam objectives
For the exam, the relevant objectives are:

* Understand database security concepts.: understanding the need to secure a database, what objects can be secured, what objects should be secured, user accounts, and roles
* Understand database backups and restore.: understanding various backup types, such as full and incremental, importance of backups, how to restore a database

Security

Introduction to database security

As IT is becoming increasingly important in this world, so is IT security. More and more valuable information gets stored, and more and more systems are connected. As a database administrator, it is your job to make sure that a user has access to the information he (or she) is authorized for, and only the data he is authorized for; no more, no less.

Unauthorized access to a company's database can have severe implications, resulting in loss of revenue, bad publicity or even bankruptcy. If you store financial information (such as credit cards), health information or customer information, you can imagine how hackers, disgruntled employees or your company's competitors might profit if they gained access to your database, changed it without your knowledge, or prevented you from accessing it.

Security is a very broad topic. It can (and should) cover many layers. For example: you can encrypt databases and hard disks; you can limit access to the database over the network; you must control physical access to the servers. These are all security measures intended to prevent hacking. Here, we'll only cover one aspect of security: giving the necessary permissions to users without giving permissions they don't need.

First, we'll tell you the concepts you need to know about security. Then, we'll show you how to perform the necessary tasks, both in T-SQL and in SSMS.

SQL authentication versus Windows authentication

By default, nobody is allowed to do anything in SQL Server until the database administrator grants them permission. Then, for every single action the person wants to perform, SQL checks whether he or she is allowed to perform that action. The first step in this process is authentication. The second step is authorization; we'll cover that next. Authentication means determining that a person actually is who he claims to be. In SQL Server, there are two possible ways to authenticate users: SQL Server authentication or Windows authentication. During installation of a SQL Server instance, you have to choose whether that instance supports either only Windows authentication, or both Windows and SQL authentication, as we've seen in chapter 1; supporting only SQL authentication is no longer possible (it was in older versions of SQL Server). Let's review both methods of authentication.

With SQL Server authentication, SQL Server stores the name and password for the person. When the person attempts to log on, he has to provide both a name and password. SQL then checks to see if the password provided by the person matches the stored password. If so, SQL decides that the person actually is who he claims to be.

With Windows authentication, SQL only stores the name. When a person attempts to log on, he does not have to enter a name and password; instead, the connection is made with the name with which he has logged on to Windows. Windows has already done the authentication, and decided that the user actually is who he claims to be; SQL trusts Windows to make that decision. In this case, Windows can either be the local server on which SQL is installed, or (preferably) Active Directory.

What is the difference between both authentication methods? Windows authentication has several advantages. First, it is more secure. There are devices and software that can intercept network communications; it is easier to extract the password from this network communication when SQL authentication is used than when Windows authentication is used. One reason for this is that Windows authentication uses stronger encryption of the communication between the client application and SQL Server; another reason is that, for Windows authentication, you can require the use of not just passwords, but the combination of a password and an additional security measure (e.g., token, smart card or fingerprint).

Second, with Windows authentication, you can take advantages of Windows groups. Instead of granting permissions to each new employee, the database administrator grants permission to a group (for instance: Researchers). When a new researcher is hired, the Windows administrators add his or her account to this Windows group, and without any work on the part of the database administrator, the new researcher receives the necessary permissions on SQL Server. Moreover: when the researcher leaves, or changes to a new position within the company, removing the account from the Windows group is enough to revoke the permissions on the database. This allows for central administration of privileges: the Windows administrators ensure that each account is a member of the correct groups, and the account will receive the correct permissions in all applications (not just SQL) without additional work on the side of the application.

On the other hand, SQL authentication has one important advantage over Windows authentication: not all applications support Windows authentication (for instance, applications that run on different operating systems). To support these applications, you need SQL authentication.

When you install a SQL instance, you decide whether to allow only Windows authentication, or both SQL and Windows authentication (this is called *mixed mode*). We've already covered the installation in chapter 1, so we'll move on to creating the logins.

Logins versus users

In SQL, there is a difference between a login and a user. First, a person has to have the permission to log in to SQL Server. At this server level, he or she is called a login. Then, he has to have permission in one or more databases. At the database level, he or she is called a user. The database administrator has to map the logon (server level) to the user (database level). It can be quite confusing when the logon is not correctly mapped to the user. You could, for instance, map user "Bert" to logon "Bob". We won't show you how to analyze or resolve this issue; we just wanted to mention this possibility to help your awareness of the difference between the logon (at the server level) and the user (at the database level).

Below is the T-SQL code sample to (a) create a login "Bob", (b) create a user with the same name and (c) map the login to the user (using T-SQL). In the code, you have to choose one of the two "create login" statements, not both.

```
USE [master]
GO
-- Windows authentication
CREATE LOGIN [Bob] FROM WINDOWS
WITH DEFAULT_DATABASE=[AdventureWorks2008R2]
-- SQL authentication
CREATE LOGIN [Bob]
WITH PASSWORD=N'VeryStrongPassword',
DEFAULT_DATABASE=[AdventureWorks2008R2]

GO
USE [AdventureWorks2008R2]
GO
CREATE USER [Bob] FOR LOGIN [Bob]
```

GO

This is how to do the same using SSMS:
* In Object Explorer, expand Security
* Right click "Logins" > New Login…
* Choose either Windows authentication or SQL authentication
* For Windows authentication: fill in the Windows account name
* For SQL authentication:
> * Fill in the user name and a password
> * Decide whether or not you need the following boxes checked:
> * Enforce password policy
> * Enforce password expiration
> * User must change password at next logon
* Specify AdventureWorks2008R2 as the default database.

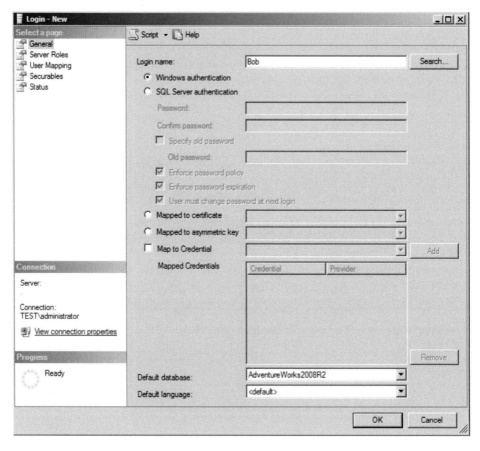

* In the left hand side of the window, click "User Mapping".
* Select the check box next to the AdventureWorks2008R2 database:

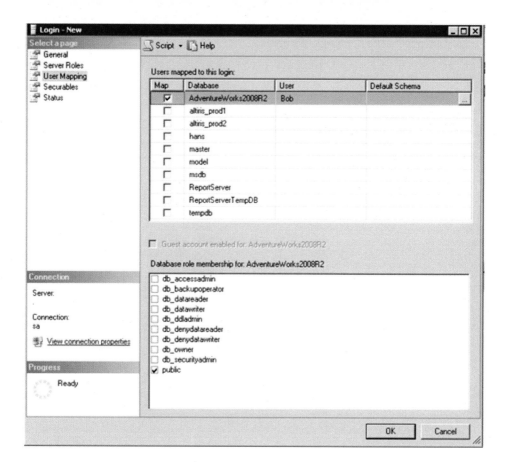

* Click OK.

By creating the user we've already moved on to the next part: authorization. Authentication means validating that the user actually is who he claims to be; authorization means assigning permissions to that user. By creating the user at the same time as the logon, we've granted the ability to connect to the database; this is authorization.

As you can see in the GUI, there are a lot of other security options. One of these options is the subject of the next part: database roles.

Roles

There are two ways to grant permission to a user: directly or through roles. A role in SQL is like a group in Windows: you grant permission to the role, add the user to the role and the users automatically receives the permissions you granted to the role. Granting permissions to a role requires less administration than granting permissions directly to all users individually.

There are several roles at both the server and database level. Server roles are beyond the scope of this exam, so we'll just mention the most important one: sysadmin. Members of the sysadmin role can do anything at the SQL Server level, and in all databases.

The most important database roles are:

* Dbo (database owner). Can do anything in the database.
* Datareader. Can read all data in all tables in the database.

* Datawriter. Can update, insert and delete in all tables in the database.

These are standard roles, but if you want to, you can make additional roles, for instance when you want more granular control.
This is how to create a role using T-SQL, and add user Bob to the role:

```
USE [AdventureWorks2008R2]
GO
CREATE ROLE [Sales]
GO
EXEC sp_addrolemember N'sales', N'Bob'
GO
```

This is how to perform the same action using SSMS:
* In Object Explorer, expand the database
* Expand security
* Right click Roles > New > New Database Role
* Enter a name for the role, and click "Add" to add Bob to this role.

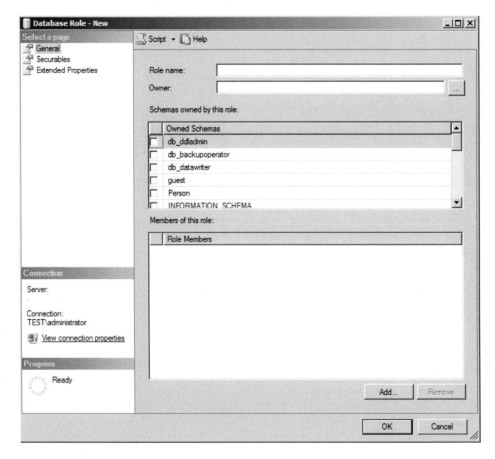

A user (or login) can belong to more than one group or role. Permissions from all different groups and roles add up, so a user receives all permissions from all groups and roles he is a member of.

Permissions

We've now created a login, and mapped it to a database user. But unless you've added the user to a database role, he is still not allowed to do anything other than log in. For that, you have to grant the user permission to perform some action on some object, for example:

```
GRANT SELECT ON [dbo].[Customers] TO [Bob];
```

In this case, we've allowed Bob to perform select statements on the Customer table. Several permissions on the same object can be granted in a single statement:

```
GRANT INSERT, UPDATE ON [dbo].[Customers] TO [Bob];
```

Each type of object has specific types of actions you can grant permission to perform. But before we continue with a list of available actions for each type of object, we'll first explain how to take permissions away.

You can grant permission using the T-SQL command "GRANT". When the user no longer needs the permission, you can take away the permission using the T-SQL command "REVOKE".

Under special circumstances, you can also deny a permission using the T-SQL command "DENY". Suppose a user belongs to a group that gives him a certain set of permissions, but there is one specific permission that should not apply to this user. For example, Bob is allowed to read all tables in the Sales schema, except for the table with profit margins. That leaves you with two options:

* Make a new group, add only this user, and grant the entire set of permissions, except the one specific permission that should not apply;
* Deny that one specific permission.

You should be very careful to deny permissions, since a deny overrules a grant. If at all possible, avoid using DENY.

That leaves us only with the specific permissions that can be granted, denied and revoked. These permissions depend on the type of object. These are the most common types of permissions for the object types we've discussed in this book:

* Table & view:
    * SELECT
    * INSERT
    * UPDATE
    * DELETE
    * ALTER
* Stored proc:
    * EXECUTE
    * ALTER

By the way: an object you can assign permissions on, is called a securable.

In chapter 4, we've created a view called vwLondonCustomers. Here's how to grant Bob to read from the view:

```
GRANT SELECT ON [dbo].[vwLondoncustomers] TO [Bob];
```

Also in chapter 4, we've created a stored procedure called procGetCustomerInformation. Here's how to grant Bob permission to run this stored proc:

```
GRANT EXEC ON [dbo].[procGetCustomerInformation] TO [Bob];
```

One caveat about granting permissions on a stored proc. Changes to stored procs can be made by either altering the stored proc, or by dropping and recreating it. With the former method, the permissions are retained; with the latter, they are not (so permissions have to be recreated).

To recap the syntax:

[Permission]	GRANT/REVOKE/DENY
[Action]	SELECT/UPDATE/DELETE/INSERT/EXEC/ALTER etc
[Securable]	ON [schema].[object]
[Principal]	TO USER/ROLE;

Now, let's perform the same task in the graphical user interface. As an example, we'll grant select on table [dbo].[Persons] to Bob.

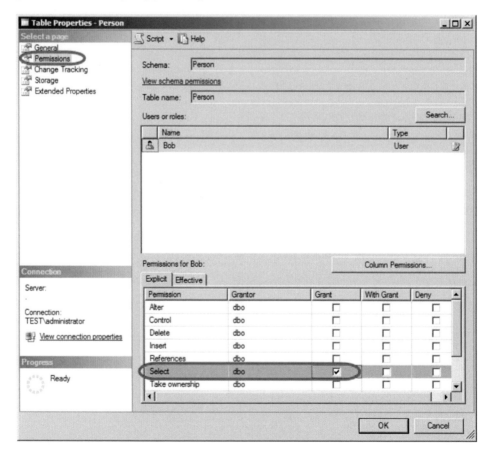

You can either go to the properties of the securable (table Persons) and add permissions to the principal (user Bob), as demonstrated in the screenshot above; or as an alternative, you can go to the properties of the principal (user Bob) and add the permissions to the securable (table Persons) there, as demonstrated in the screenshot below.

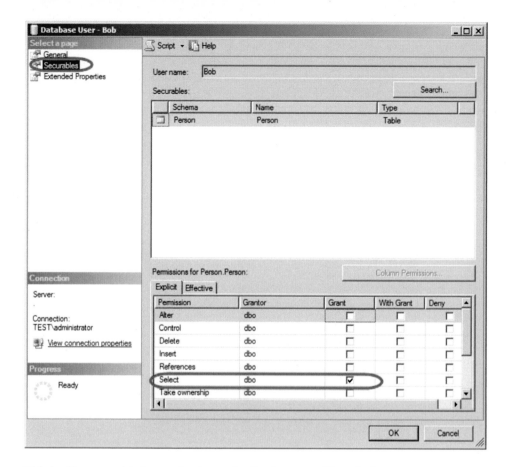

This is all you need to know about security for the exam. There is, however, one additional thing we find worth mentioning: SQL injection. This is a commonly used hacking technique.

Image a web site where web users can view their orders by entering an order number on a web form. The web application could retrieve the necessary information by blindly adding the order number to the following query:

```
SELECT *
FROM   Orders
WHERE  OrderID  = ...
```

Without any input validation, this can go wrong pretty quickly when a hacker would, instead of entering just an order number, enter a number followed by a valid SQL statement. For example, the hacker could enter "1; drop table orders". The query would then simply become:

```
SELECT *
FROM   Orders
WHERE  OrderID  = 1; DROP TABLE Orders
```

Given the required permissions, both statements would be executed, causing severe damage to the database. Probably, the web application does not need the permission to drop the table, so it shouldn't have that permission (either granted explicitly or because the web application user is member of the dbo role, database owner). But even if the web application needs dbo permissions (for some other actions than this simple select), there are several ways to prevent this SQL injection. Input validation on the part of the web application is one; using stored procedures on the side of the database is another. In chapter 4, we said that stored procs can be used for security purposes; this example demonstrates the extra security stored procs can provide. The stored proc to prevent SQL injection might look like this:

```
CREATE PROC procGetOrder
        @order INT
AS
BEGIN
        SELECT *
        FROM    Orders
        WHERE   OrderID = @order;
END
GRANT EXEC procGetOrder to WebAppUser
```

Since "1; drop table orders" is not an integer, this hack attempt would not work. Creating a stored procedure for every possible action, and then granting the appropriate permissions, takes a lot more development effort than simply granting the web application database owner permissions. But it is, as you can see, much safer. Still, you should use input validation on the part of the web application as well; security should be a multi layered approach. This example is meant to demonstrate one very common type of attack on a database, and to demonstrate the importance of good security. With this example, we conclude our part about security.

Backup and restore

Introduction
Making backups is the most important task for a database administrator. Or to be more precise: ensuring the ability to restore a database. If something happens to your database, and you're unable to restore all data, the consequences for your company can be quite expensive. In many companies, loss of several days of production data can mean bankruptcy.
In the SQL injection example at the end of the previous section, you'd have to restore the database to retrieve the dropped Orders table. Without a backup, the contents of the Orders table would permanently be lost. A dropped table is one reason to restore a database; other possible reasons are, for example, a crashed server, archiving needs or creating a copy for testing or development purposes.
In this section, we'll talk about backups. First, we'll discuss the available types of backups. Then, we'll discuss the business aspects you need to know to design an appropriate backup strategy using these types of backups. Finally, we'll show you how to perform the actual backup, and perform a restore.

Backup types
There are several types of backups. The most common types are:
* Full backup;
* Differential backup;

* Transaction log backups.

There are other types, but these are beyond the scope of the exam.

The first type of backup we're going to discuss is the full backup. A full backup contains the whole database. All data, all object definitions and all user information is contained in the full backup. A restore process always begins with the restore of a full backup, regardless of whether you want to restore additional backups (differential or transaction log backups). Restoring a full backup is an all-or-nothing procedure; you can't restore just a part of the database. There are, however, third party tools that provide this functionality (e.g. from RedGate and ApexSQL).

The second type of backup is the differential backup. A differential backup contains everything that has changed since the last full backup. To restore a differential backup, you first have to restore a full backup (usually the most recent), followed by the latest differential backup. If you have taken multiple differential backups after the most recent full backup, you only need to restore the last differential backup (if you restore all differential backups, the result is the same as restoring only the last differential backup, it just takes longer). As with the full backup, restoring a differential backup is an all-or-nothing process.

The advantage of taking a differential backup is that, because it only contains the changes, taking a differential backup is usually faster than a full backup, and the resulting backup file is smaller. The disadvantage is that you need both a full backup and a differential backup to be able to restore; therefore, the total restore process takes longer.

The third type of backup is the transaction log backup. A transaction log backup contains every change since the previous transaction log backup. To restore a transaction log, you'd have to restore the latest full backup, followed by every single transaction log backup taken since that full backup. If you also take differential backups, you would first restore the full backup, then either:
* the latest differential backup followed by every transaction log backup since the differential backup;
* or every single transaction log since the latest full backup.

The former is usually faster than restoring every log backup since the latest full backup. The most important advantage of transaction backups is that they allow for point in time recovery. With both full backups and differential backups, you have to restore the entire backup; with transaction log backups, you can choose to restore only part of the backup. For example, if a table is dropped at 16:08:00, and the last transaction log backup has been made at 16:15, you can restore the database to the exact state of 16:07:59.

Taking a full backup has no impact on the contents of the next transaction log backup; it *does* change the content of the next differential backup.

In SQL Server, there is no separate incremental backup, although this term is sometimes used for a transaction log backup (for instance, in the exam objectives for this topic). The most important disadvantage of transaction log backups is that the database has to retain every single change until you perform the transaction log backup. This has to do with the database recovery model. There are three database recovery models: full, simple and bulk logged. The difference between those models is the amount of changes that are kept in the transaction log file (as you'll remember from chapter 1, this is one of the two files that are part of every database; the other is the data file). In all models, every change is written first to the log file before it is written to the data file. The difference between those models is what happens after the change has been written to both files. In the simple recovery model, as soon as a change is written to the data file, it is removed from the log file. In the full recovery model, the change is kept in the log file until a log backup is made. The bulk logged model is similar to the full model, with one exception: changes can be grouped together in operations known as bulk logged operations; those changes can only be recovered as a group, but all other changes are handled the same as in the full recovery model.

To be able to take a transaction log backup, the transaction log file has to contain those changes, therefore the database has to be in either the full or the bulk logged model. This means that the log file will grow larger than it would in the simple recovery model. And if, for whatever reason, the log backups aren't being performed anymore, the log will keep growing until it can't grow any further (i.e., the disk is full or the maximum file size has been reached).

Backup strategy

A sounds backup strategy has to take into account at least the following aspects:
* The time it takes to restore a backup;
* The overhead of the backup process on the server;
* The retention period;
* The amount of space the backup files take up;
* The amount of data you are willing to lose for that particular database.

We'll cover these aspects in more detail.

By the way: this backup strategy is not something you, as an IT professional, should decide upon on your own, but rather something that has to be agreed upon by the IT apartment and the responsible data owners in the business.

The maximum amount of time it should take to restore a backup is often called the Recovery Time Objective (RTO). This includes the time to restore the full backup and if applicable, a differential backup and one or more transaction log backups. Quite often, backups are stored on a file share and subsequently moved to tape; in that case, the backup file would first have to be recovered from tape, and the necessary time to do that is included in the RTO. This RTO is important, because the database will be unavailable during the period of the restore.

The overhead of the backup process can be a very practical problem, and becomes more important as the database grows large. A full backup has to read the entire database, and write it to a backup file; a differential database has to read the entire database as well, and write all changed pages to the backup file. Both can create substantial amounts of disk IO. To give an example: depending on the type of hardware used, a full backup of a 100 GB database to a network file share might take an hour. During this hour, the performance of other processes on the database may be degraded. It is best to find a time frame during which there is low activity, but for some applications, there might not be such a time frame.

The retention period determines how long you have to preserve the backups before deleting them. Often, legal requirements determine how long data has to be preserved. This doesn't necessarily mean you have to preserve your backups for that period of time, as data is preserved inside the database. For example: preserving 7 years of daily full backups might not be a good idea, as this will take up a lot of space. Therefore, you have to decide upon a mix of preserving data in the database, and preserving database backups.

Retention period is a big factor in the next aspect on the list: the amount of space the backup files take up. Other factors are the size of the databases, the frequency of the backups and the type of backup. Backups can be made to disk or to tape. Tape is often less expensive than disk, but slower to make backups to, and restore backups from.

Quite often, a mix of disk and tape is used: backups are first made to disk (with a short retention period), and those backups are backed up to tape (with a longer retention period).

The final aspect on the list is the amount of data the business is willing to lose. This is often referred to as the Recovery Point Objective: the point in time just before the disaster, up to which the database can be restored. The latest point up to which you can restore is the time of the last backup file you have available. This is not necessarily the time of the last backup you made; if you make a backup to the same disk that houses the database itself, you might lose both the backup and the database at the same time. Therefore, you need to make backups to a different device (server, file share, tape drive) than the database server itself.

These are the aspects that should determine your backup strategy. For the MTA 98-364 exam, you have to design that backup strategy using just full backups, differential backups and log backups. In the real world, there are more types of backup, and all sorts of different tools to choose from.

* A commonly used backup strategy might look something like this:
* A full backup every week;
* A differential backup every day;
* A transaction log backup every 15 minutes.

Performing a backup

You can perform a database backup using the graphical user interface, or using T-SQL statements. In this example, we'll use SSMS to create a backup script. Right click on the database of which you want to make a backup. In the "Back Up Database" screen, you specify the following:
* The database you want to back up;
* The backup type:
* Full;
* Differential;
* Transaction log.

* For a full database backup: whether or not to make a copy-only backup. As stated, a full backup has impact on a subsequent differential backup: a differential backup only contains those database pages that have been marked as changed. Normally, a full backup resets this page as "not changed"; a copy-only backup does not perform this reset. This is useful if you want to perform a backup outside of the regular schedule.
* Whether to make a database backup or a file backup. Backups of files and filegroups are beyond the scope of this exam.
* The backup destination. The default extension for a backup file is bak. A backup file can contain multiple backups; if you're going to restore to an existing backup file, click Contents to view the backups already contained in that file.

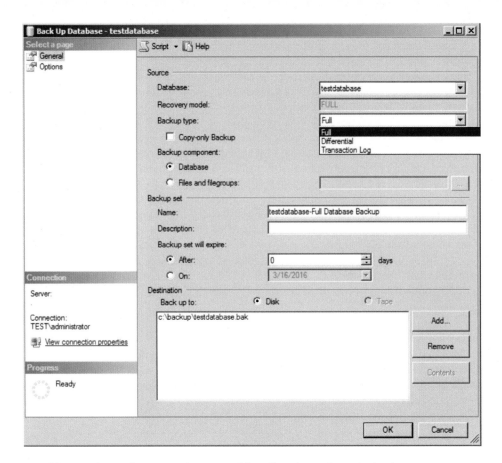

We'll ignore the Options page. You can either directly perform the backup, or create a script.

A few final words on backups, before we move on to restores. As a database administrator, you need to make daily backups of all your databases. Obviously, you are not going to do this manually; you would create maintenance plans or automated SQL jobs to do this. You should also check the results of these jobs daily, and periodically perform test restores. If there is something wrong with your backup strategy, or its implementation, you really need to know this (and fix this) before you need to perform an actual restore.

Restoring a backup

Compared to the backup, performing a restore is relatively easy. Performing a backup requires you to make a lot of choices, some of which we have covered previously. When performing a restore, your options are limited by the backups you actually have available.

For the exam, you only need to know three types of backup: full, differential and transaction log, so these are the restores we'll cover. When these are the only types of backup you have available, a restore involves at least two steps:

* restoring a full backup;
* performing recovery.

The restore process always starts with the restore of a full backup. The restore process ends with recovery; this is the process whereby SQL rolls back transactions that were being performed at the time the full backup was started, but were not completed before the backup was finished. This recovery process is necessary to put the database in a consistent state, and make it available to users.

An example of T-SQL code to perform a restore is:

```
RESTORE DATABASE [testdatabase]
FROM DISK = 'F:\backups\testdatabase.bak';
```

This accomplishes both steps, the full restore and the recovery, since recovery is the default. If you do not want SQL to automatically recover the database, you have to instruct it not to do so. In the next code sample, we've split these two steps into two separate commands:

```
RESTORE DATABASE [testdatabase]
FROM DISK = 'F:\backups\dbTest.bak'
WITH NORECOVERY;

RESTORE DATABASE [testdatabase]
WITH RECOVERY;
```

The combined effect of these two statements is the same as the single restore statement above, but is allows us to do something in between; we'll get to that.

By the way: the database you're trying to restore, should either be deleted before the restore, or by the restore process itself (using the keywords WITH REPLACE). And to be able to delete the database, it should not be in use; if it is in use, you should drop all existing connections first.

In between the two steps of restore and recover, you can restore additional backups: differential and/or transaction log backups. You can only restore additional backups when recovery has not yet been performed. This makes sense. As mentioned above, recovery rolls back the transactions that were not yet finished when the backup ended. Let's assume that a transaction started during the full backup, and ended somewhere before or during the subsequent transaction log backup. Part of the transaction is then contained in the full backup, and the remaining part of the transaction is contained in the transaction log backup. If you remember from our discussion of transactions, a transaction is all or nothing, never partial.

So if you only restore the full backup, the finished result should not reflect any part of the transaction that wasn't finished at the time the backup finished; the part of the transaction that is contained in the full backup must be removed (in database terminology: rolled back). If you restore both the full backup and the subsequent transaction log backup, the finished result *must* reflect the entire transaction. Obviously, this would be impossible if the part of the transaction that is contained in the full backup had been removed during recovery; therefore, recovery only runs after all restores have been performed, making subsequent restores impossible.

So the restore process starts with a full restore, and ends with recovery. In between, you can restore differential and/or transaction log backups.

A differential backup contains the result of all changes since the previous full backup. You only have to restore a single differential backup; there is no point restoring more than one (though you could, if you wanted to). Example: let's say you perform a full backup on Sunday, and a differential backup every other night. On Friday afternoon, the

database server crashes. You repair the server, and need to restore the database to the latest time possible. These are the steps you need to perform:
* Restore the full backup from Sunday (with NORECOVERY);
* Restore the differential backup from Thursday (with NORECOVERY);
* Perform recovery.

In this case, you've lost all changes to the database since the last differential backup on Thursday night.
If you do not want to risk losing so many changes, you should make transaction log backups regularly. A transaction log backup contains all the changes since the last transaction log backup. Therefore, you have to restore *all* transaction log backups that have been made since the last full or differential backup you've restored, in the order they have been made. Should one of the transaction log backups be missing, or corrupt, the restore process ends there.
Let's use the same example (Sunday full backups and daily differential backups), but now you have also scheduled a transaction log backup every hour. Now, in order to restore the database to the latest time possible, these are the steps you need to perform:
* Restore the full backup from Sunday (with NORECOVERY);
* Restore the differential backup from Thursday (again, with NORECOVERY);
* Restore all transaction log backups since the differential backup from Thursday (with NORECOVERY);
* Perform recovery.

With transaction log backups, you can perform a point-in-time restore. This can be useful when, for example, somebody has inadvertently dropped a table, or executed an update statement but forgot the WHERE clause. In that case, you do not want to restore the database to the latest time possible, but to the moment just prior to the mistake. To perform a point-in-time restore, use the clause STOPAT:

```
RESTORE LOG [testdatabase]
FROM DISK = 'F:\backups\testdatabase.trn'
WITH STOPAT = '2015-02-09 17:53:00';
```

This means that, unlike the full backup and the differential backup, you do not need to restore a transaction log completely. Obviously, this only applies to the last transaction log you're going to restore; after STOPAT you can't restore any more logs.
This concludes our overview of database backups.

Summary

In this chapter, we've covered security and backup & restore.
On the topic of security, we've talked about the difference between Windows and SQL authentication. We've demonstrated how to create a logon at the server level, and match it to a user at the database level, both in T-SQL and the GUI. We've also demonstrated how to give, revoke and deny permissions to a role or user. We've discussed the following best practices:
* whenever possible, assign permissions to groups, not to individual accounts;
* Windows authentication is more secure than SQL authentication, because of encryption and centralized management of group membership;
* assign only the permissions needed to get the job done, no more.

On the topic of backup and restore, we've talked about the different type of backups (full, differential and transaction log) and how you can use them to formulate a backup strategy.

Further reading

Microsoft has provided a detailed set of security best practices. For every version of SQL Server, you can find a whitepaper on the Microsoft web site.
As stated in the section on backups, you should perform at least daily backups for your databases. You're not going to do that manually, but by using Maintenance Plans or SQL Server scripts. Using a wizard in SSMS, you can set up Maintenance Plans to create and schedule jobs that perform backups and other maintenance tasks such as reorganizing indexes and database consistency checks. Maintenance Plans are easy to set up, and therefore a good way to start. But if you want more granular control over the process, take a look at the excellent scripts of Ola Hallengren (these scripts are available for free on his web site, https://ola.hallengren.com/).

Questions

QUESTION 1
By default, a user in a database has only read permissions, until an administrator grants him or her additional permissions.

A True
B False

QUESTION 2
You take daily full backups, and transaction log backups (every hour on the hour). After somebody accidentally dropped the database on Tuesday 14:17, you need to restore the database, minimizing data loss. You discover the backup file of Monday night is corrupt. Can you use the backup file of Sunday night to restore the database to the state of 14:16 on Tuesday?

A Yes, you can restore the database without data loss.
B Yes, but then you can only restore the transaction logs to the point of the Monday night full backup.
C No, after the Monday night backup, the Sunday night backup has become invalid. You should have taken differential backups for this scenario.
D No, you can only restore to 14:00.

QUESTION 3
You work in a company with three departments: accounting, manufacturing and management. Your SQL server has two databases: one with accounting information and one with sales information. Each department needs read and write access to its own database. Management needs full access to both databases. How do you set up permissions?

A Create a login for each user. Add each user to the appropriate database. Assign the management user to dbo role in each database, and other users to both the datareader and datawriter role in the appropriate database.
B Create a login for each user. Add each user to the appropriate database. Assign the management user to the sysadminrole, and other users to both the datareader and datawriter role in the appropriate database.
C Create a Windows group for each department. Add a login for each group. Assign the management group to sysadmin role in each database, and other users to both the datareader and datawriter role in the appropriate database.
D Create a Windows group for each department. Add a login for each group. Assign the management group to dbo role in each database, and the other logins to both the datareader and datawriter role in the appropriate database.

QUESTION 4
What is a good reason to perform differential backups?

A Better RTO
B Faster backup
C Point in time recovery
D Backup encryption

QUESTION 5
What statement is true about recovery?

A Recovery is needed to restore additional backups
B Recovery is done after every backup
C Recovery only applies to full backups
D Recovery must be done before users can access the database

QUESTION 6
You have a HR table with sensitive information. Junior HR employees are allowed to some attributes of the table, while only some senior employees should receive access to the whole table. How can you accomplish this?

A Create a view that selects only the required columns from the HR table. Grant the logons of the junior HR employees read permissions on this view.
B Create a custom database role for junior HR employees. Create a stored proc that selects only the required rows from the HR table. Grant exec permissions on this stored proc to the junior HR role.
C Create a Windows group for junior HR employees. Create a function that returns only the nonsensitive information. Grant permissions on the function to the junior HR Windows group.
D Create a Windows group for junior HR employees. Grant read permissions to this group on the nonsensitive attributes of the table.

QUESTION 7
Every Saturday evening, you perform a full backup, every other evening, a differential backup, and log backups every 15 minutes. On Wednesday 17:23, the server crashes. You restore the full backup with NORECOVERY. How should you proceed to restore the database with minimum data loss?

A Restore all available differential backups. Next, restore all log backups since Tuesday evening.
B Restore the differential backup of Tuesday. Next, restore all log backups since Tuesday evening.
C Restore all available differential backups. Next, restore all log backups.
D Restore all available differential backups. Next, restore the latest transaction log backup.
E This cannot be done, as the full restore should have been done without recovery.

QUESTION 8
All employees from the sales department are allowed read access to the sales database, but only some employees from the sales department (Buyers) are allowed read access to the [Purchase] table. You propose the following permissions:
* Create a Windows group for sales employees, and add this group to the datareader database role
* Revoke permissions for this group on the Purchase table
* Create a second Windows group for Buyers. Grant this group read permissions on the Purchase table.

Will this solution work?

A Yes
B No

QUESTION 9
What is not an advantage of Windows authentication over SQL authentication?

A Windows authentication is more secure than SQL authentication through better encryption.
B Windows authentication allows for better separation of duties with regards to user administration than SQL authentication.
C Windows authentication allows complexity rules for passwords, while SQL authentication does not.

QUESTION 10
Which database recovery model allows for transaction log back-ups?

A Simple
B Full
C Log insert
D All of the above

Answers

This section contains the correct answers to the questions, plus an explanation of the wrong answers. In addition to the correct answers, we'll also give a few pointers which are useful on the actual exam.

QUESTION 1
The correct answer is B: false. A user has no permissions until an administrator grants permissions, not even read access. This is called secure by default.

QUESTION 2
The correct answer is D. As your last transaction log backup has been performed on 14:00, this is the latest point you can restore to. Therefore, answer A is incorrect. The full backup taken on Monday night has no effect on either the full backup of Sunday, or the transaction log backups; therefore, answers B and C are incorrect.

QUESTION 3
The correct answer is: D. Creating a logon for each individual user is not necessary. While this is, in itself, not enough to eliminate answers A and B there is probably a better answer. Assigning logons to the sysadmin role gives them far too much rights; therefore, answers B and C are incorrect. While the solution of answer A would work, the solution of answer D would be easier to implement and maintain. Therefore, the correct answer is D.

QUESTION 4
The correct answer is B: faster backup. Because a differential backup is usually smaller than a full backup, backup time is shorter. Restore time however is longer, therefore A is not correct. A differential backup does not facilitate point in time recovery, you need transaction log backups for that; therefore, C is incorrect. And whether or not you can perform backup encryption depends upon the version and edition of SQL Server, not on the type of backup; therefore, D is not correct.

QUESTION 5
The correct answer is D. Recovery is performed after the last restore, whether the last restore is a full, differential or transaction log restore, in order to roll back the uncommitted transactions in the backup. Therefore, answers A, B and C are incorrect.

QUESTION 6
The correct answer is A. Answer B is incorrect, as the stored proc filters rows, not columns. Answer C is incorrect, as a function is not appropriate in this situation. Answer D is incorrect, as you cannot directly grant permissions on part of a table (not in current versions of SQL, anyway).
The answers also differ in the principals that receive permissions. Answer A will have you granting permissions directly on individual accounts, which is not a best practice. It is better to grant permissions to a group, and preferably a Windows group; however, because the solutions of answers B, C and D will not work, this extra information is irrelevant.

QUESTION 7
The correct answer is B. After the full backup, you restore the last differential backup, and every transaction log after the last differential backup. Alternatively, you could

restore every transaction log, but that answer was not given. Answer E is wrong, because recovery should only be done after the last restore.

QUESTION 8
The correct answer is B: no. Part of the solution is that you try to revoke permissions on the Purchase table, but these permissions have not been granted. A "deny" instead of "revoke" would work, though.

QUESTION 9
The correct answer is C. Both Windows and SQL authentication allow for password complexity rules. The other statements are true.

QUESTION 10
The correct answer is B: full recovery model. The simple recovery model only allows for full backups and differential backups, not transaction log backups as entries in the log file can be overwritten as soon as the transaction is written to the database file. There is no "insert log" recovery model. There is another recovery model that allows for transaction log backups, the bulk logged model, but that is not an available answer.

Glossary

Authentication
The process whereby a computer determines whether the user actually is whom he or she claims to be. In SQL Server, this process can either be done by SQL Server itself (through the combination of a user name and password), or be left to Windows (using the Windows account). The former is called SQL Authentication; the latter Windows Authentication.

Authorization
The process whereby SQL Server grants permission to an already authenticated logon. By default, no permissions are granted; therefore, an account has no permissions until the database administrator explicitly grants permissions to that account, or a group that account belongs to.

Candidate key
In normalization, an attribute (or combination of attributes) that uniquely identifies a row. For a combination of attributes to be considered a candidate key, it has to be the *smallest* possible subset of attributes to uniquely identify a row; if you can remove an attribute from a certain subset of attributes and the remaining subset can still uniquely identify a row, the larger subset of attributes is not a candidate key.

Collation
Collation determines the sort order and comparison of characters. For example, one difference between collations is whether it is case sensitive or case insensitive. In a case insensitive collation, "e" equals "E", but in a case sensitive database, "e" does not equal "E"; in an accent insensitive database, "e" equals "é", but in an accent sensitive database, it does not.

DDL
Data Definition Language. The collective term for T-SQL commands change the definition of the objects (e.g. tables), not the data: for example: CREATE, DROP and ALTER. The other major category is DML, Data Manipulation Language; this is the collective term for T-SQL commands that manipulate the data.

DML
Data Manipulation Language. The collective term for T-SQL commands that manipulate the data: for example, INSERT, UPDATE, DELETE and (depending on who you ask) SELECT. The other major category is DDL, Data Definition language; this is the collective term for T-SQL commands that change the definition of the objects (e.g. tables), not the data.

Foreign key
A foreign key is an attribute in a table that points to an attribute in another table (often the primary key). Example: CustomerID in an Orders table that points to the CustomerID attribute of the Customers table.

GUI

Graphical User Interface, the graphical way to interact with a program. The alternative method to interact with a program is the command line. For SQL Server, the GUI is usually SSMS.

Instance
A SQL Server instance is a separate installation of SQL Server. Each instance has its own databases, binaries, processes, administrators, and network port(s). SQL Server 2008 R2 supports 50 instances on a single server.

Intellisense
The Management Studio version of auto correct. As you type, Intellisense will color code keywords, offer suggestions for you to complete (using TAB) and underline incorrect syntax.

Normal form
A normal form formally describes a level of normalization. Each level of normalization eliminates additional redundancy. Five levels of normalization have been defined (called first normal form or 1NF, second normal form or 2NF etc.). A database is said to be in a certain normal form when the database design conforms to the rules for that normal form (in addition to all lower normal forms).

Normalization
Normalization is the process of organizing the attributes and tables, in order to achieve an appropriate level of data redundancy. The result of normalization is a logical database design of tables, their attributes and relationships between these tables.

Null
Unknown value.

Primary key
A primary key is a column (or set of columns) that uniquely identifies a record in a table.

RDBMS
Relational Database System. A system that manages relational databases, such as Oracle Database, Microsoft SQL Server or IBM DB2. An RDBMS includes not only the relational database, but also the memory processes needed to control access to the physical database files.

RPO
Recovery Point Objective: the point in time to which a given database can be restored from the available backups. This is an indication of the amount of data that could be lost in the case of an emergency.

RTO
Recovery Time Objective. The amount of time it takes to restore a backup for a given database.

Scalar
A variable that can hold only a single value at a time.

Schema

A schema is a container for database objects. All objects belong to one and only one schema. By default, there is only one schema in a database: dbo. Schemas can be used to group objects and apply security.

Service pack

A service pack is a bundle of bug fixes (called patches).

SSMS

SQL Server Management Studio. The main program for SQL Server administration.

Stored procedure

A stored procedure is a small T-SQL program stored inside the database: this can be a single T-SQL statement, or a collection of statements.

T-SQL

See Transact SQL

Transact SQL

Transact SQL, or T-SQL, is a superset of the ANSI standard Structured Query Language. This means that, besides the standard SQL language, T-SQL contains extra commands that are specific to SQL Server.

Triggers

A trigger is a special type of stored procedure that is automatically executed after a defined event occurs in the database.
There are three types of triggers: DML, DDL and logon triggers. The difference is the type of event that has to happen to fire the trigger.

Made in the USA
Coppell, TX
27 August 2020